9-78857

GUIDANCE MONOGRAPH SERIES

Series VI: Minority Groups and Guidance

Counseling Negroes

Clemmont E. Vontress

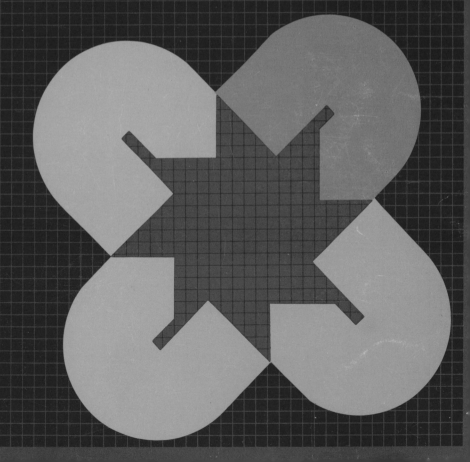

GUIDANCE MONOGRAPH SERIES

SHELLEY C. STONE

BRUCE SHERTZER

Editors

GUIDANCE MONOGRAPH SERIES

The general purpose of Houghton Mifflin's Guidance Monograph Series is to provide high quality coverage of topics which are of abiding importance in contemporary counseling and guidance practice. In a rapidly expanding field of endeavor, change and innovation are inevitably present. A trend accompanying such growth is greater and greater specialization. Specialization results in an increased demand for materials which reflect current modifications in guidance practice while simultaneously treating the field in greater depth and detail than commonly found in textbooks and brief journal articles.

The list of eminent contributors to this series assures the reader expert treatment of the areas covered. The monographs are designed for consumers with varying familiarity to the counseling and guidance field. The editors believe that the series will be useful to experienced practitioners as well as beginning students. While these groups may use the monographs with somewhat different goals in mind, both will benefit from the treatment given to content areas.

The content areas treated have been selected because of specific criteria. Among them are timeliness, practicality, and persistency of the issues involved. Above all, the editors have attempted to select topics which are of major substantive concern to counseling and guidance personnel.

Shelley C. Stone

Bruce Shertzer

COUNSELING

NEGROES

CLEMMONT E. VONTRESS

GEORGE WASHINGTON UNIVERSITY

HOUGHTON MIFFLIN COMPANY · BOSTON

NEW YORK · ATLANTA · GENEVA, ILL. · DALLAS · PALO ALTO

ISBN: 0–395–12048–9
Library of Congress Catalog Card
Number: 79–141289

CONTENTS

EDITORS' INTRODUCTION

This monograph, *Counseling Negroes*, can relieve counselors and others of many of their misconceptions about black clients. Clemmont Vontress offers astute observations on the black-white and black-black counselor relationship and on the process and procedures of counseling. Vontress has a refreshing ability to cut through to the issues . . . and the issues involve people. He draws conclusions that he believes should influence counseling provided to black people.

Some counselors, along with many other professionals, are just beginning to understand the difficulty and complexity involved in helping blacks. Vontress has concluded that, despite external criticism and struggles within the counseling profession, counseling practitioners can, and indeed must, respond to the challenge that lies before them. He does not conclude, nor do the editors, that counseling alone can solve all of the problems created by pervasive social ills. His major thesis is that a better understanding of the origin, nature, and effects of the many influences on the behavior of blacks can serve as a base for effective counseling.

We believe that this monograph is well worth careful study. Every counselor should read it, as should anyone who seeks a better grasp of how helping relationships can become more meaningful. Understanding and acting upon the author's suggestions would do much to enable counselors to achieve their professional goals and personal ideals.

SHELLEY C. STONE

BRUCE SHERTZER

AUTHOR'S INTRODUCTION

The writing of this monograph has been an enjoyable experience, probably because a subject of personal research for nearly fifteen years has assumed such general interest. *Counseling Negroes* does not pretend to answer all of the questions which have been raised by counselors since the beginning of the so-called Negro Revolution. The problems inherent in counseling blacks in this country are so complex that it would be foolhardy to suggest that a prescription could be crammed into a single monograph or book.

An attempt is made to introduce counselors to some of the racial and cultural barriers which they may encounter in counseling blacks of all ages. Apologies may be in order for providing more questions than answers. But each day's research and consideration of the subject brings new questions or fresh difficulties with old problems. Even with these limitations, counselors and other professionals should find this monograph a handy source of reference.

Acknowledgement is due to the many individuals who were involved in bringing this monograph to completion. First, the *Guidance Monograph Series* editors, Drs. Shertzer and Stone, provided the invitation and encouragement to write it. Second, the author's colleagues at George Washington University gave advice and assistance in its composition. Finally, Mrs. Jacqueline ("Jackie") Waters, girl Friday, offered her time to bring the manuscript to acceptable form.

CLEMMONT E. VONTRESS

1

Reason for Concern

The title of this monograph is *Counseling Negroes*. Counseling, as used here, refers to an interpersonal relationship between two or more individuals, one of whom is perceived as being able to help the other(s) in some way. The aim of the counselor is to assist the counselee to adjust to his environment or environments. This definition incorporates the idea of group counseling as well as the usual dyad. Although, desirably, the helper should be professionally trained to assist the counselee, the most important aspect of the relationship is the perception which the counselee has of the helper. Thus, the word *perceived* is a significant delineation.

The purpose of the relationship is to help the counselee to achieve and/or maintain adjustment to his environment(s). Adjustment is a dynamic process. No one is completely well-adjusted, except perhaps the dead person. Also, individuals live not just in one environment but move from one to another daily; there are the home, work, social, and educational environments. One can be "well-adjusted" in one setting and not so in another. Therefore, perforce, the counselor is concerned with the individual's total experiences in all of his overlapping environments.

Negroes, the second word in the title, refers to individuals of African descent who were born and reared in this country. The word *black* is not used, because it carries a psychological connotation. As currently used, it refers not to the color of skin, but to a state of mind, a feeling about one's minority status. Implied in the racial designation *black* is the idea that the person so named is proud of his racial heritage, that he no longer hates himself, either because of skin color or other physiological features. It suggests further that the person demanding that he be referred to as such is using the defense mechanism, reaction formation. In effect, he is switching the meaning of the word, which, until a few years ago, was a fighting word when used as a racial designation. The word *colored* is not used, because today it has among many people of African descent a connotation more derogatory than *Negro*. Derived from the French phrase "gens de couleur" (mulatto), it suggests to blacks the deplorable hybridization inflicted upon people of African descent by white slave masters. That is a part of the past that many black people would rather forget. Although *black* appears to be officially in vogue, the vast majority of those of African descent still prefer to be called *Negro*. Thus, the title, *Counseling Negroes*, is perhaps the most neutral, if not the most appropriate, at this stage of the semantic hassle. However, for stylistic reasons the words *black* and *Negro* are used interchangeably throughout this monograph.

Why the Concern?

That counseling is counseling has been the attitude of some people in the profession. This position implies that individuals are more alike than they are unlike. Little recognition is taken of the many differences found among people in a society such as ours. In retrospect, counselor education of the forties and fifties may be described as a cookbook approach to helping people. That the recipe did not result in the same product for all people was not of crucial concern. Some counselors became so proficient in their art that they hardly found it necessary to interview a client in order to know his problem. This was especially true of those who used diagnostic constructs and relied heavily on tests and other data. Although the profession has always emphasized the importance of recognizing the uniqueness of each individual, counselor educators have continued to train individuals as if they would be counseling individuals who come from a society in which everybody is socially and culturally alike.

America is composed of a multitude of ethnic, racial, and regional subcultures with which people identify and from which they derive many distinctive values and norms. Each group considers its way of life natural and the best way. Strange groups, beliefs, and practices are often suspect merely because they are strange. Although a part of the larger society, these groups form cultural communities. The extent to which they are excluded from full participation in the larger society appears to be the extent to which they are alienated from that total society.

Today, there are four major minorities which constitute cultural islands in this country. They are the American Indians, the Spanish heritage group, the Appalachian whites, and the American Negroes. The largest minority group is the 20 million blacks. They, like the other groups, are not only isolated from the majority group, but are also culturally and psychologically different as compared to the dominant group. The majority of them, over 70 percent, live in the great cities, to which they have migrated during the last fifty years. During this time, they have constantly sought integration into the mainstream of the society, but with little avail. Having been schooled in the melting pot tradition, they sought that goal only to discover that black does not melt.

Not only are Negroes outside the melting pot, but what is worse, they are victims of a system of pernicious racism that exists throughout the country (Harrington, 1967). Its mechanisms are economic and social: a labor market that keeps them at the lowest levels of income and skill, a housing market that confines them to racial ghettos, and an educational process that produces more dropouts than high school graduates. It is understandable that many of them are hostile Americans.

Although whites and blacks have lived and worked together since their arrival on this continent, they are more divided physically and psychologically today than ever before in the history of this country. During the 17th and 18th centuries, blacks and whites, although masters and slaves, lived in close proximity. In many cases, they went to church together, attended the same schools, lived in the same houses, and often cohabited.

It seems ironical that the more equal blacks become, the more apart they become from whites, many of whom continue to view them as phobogenic objects (Fanon, 1967). It is understandable that today blacks tend to regroup and to consider anew their plight in America. In the process of regrouping, they have switched the meaning of the word *black*, and they have developed an ethos of their own. "Soul" is an interesting example of this phenomenon. Crudely defined, it stands for the essence of Negroness. Soul implies total acceptance of all things Negro — music, food, dress, behavior, and the like — and a tacit rejection of everything white.

The new black attitude communicates itself to whites as anger, hostility, and rejection. Majority group people who once thought that they could relate harmoniously with blacks are now getting the message that they are not wanted, that they are the enemy. Whites are now asking questions about their ability to relate to Negroes. All over the country, whites, especially responsible leaders in large organizations and government agencies, are instituting massive in-service training programs in an effort to learn to relate to the Negro again.

Counselors are also concerned about their ability to relate to blacks. For the last four or five APGA conventions, program presenters have been bombarded with questions posed by white counselors about their ability to counsel black students. Indeed, counselors find themselves in a dilemma, for they have been trained to deal with the modal adolescent population and now find something missing. Although their training may put them in good stead with colored people and middle-class Negroes, they are completely at a loss when dealing with young blacks on high school and college campuses.*

Some Counseling Settings

Pervasive racial attitudes in the society spill over into all social systems where counselors work, potentially contaminating counseling relationships. Undoubtedly, counselors in educational settings — elementary, high school and college — are most dramatically affected, because they constitute the largest body of counselors in the country and because they are working with the most vocal and expressive age group.

The shifting of racial attitudes also affects counselors working in the Work Incentive Program, the United States Training and Employment Service, Equal Employment Opportunity counselors in all governmental agencies, welfare agencies, and those who work in penal institutions, just to mention a few settings where government counselors function. In an effort to bridge the "racial barrier," many governmental agencies have launched intensive in-service training programs for their counselors, the majority of whom are not as professionally trained as school counselors.

Strained Rapport: The Basic Problem

Rapport refers to the harmonious relationship existing between the counselor and the counselee in a counseling dyad or to the existence

---

* Here, a distinction is made between blacks (persons of African descent who express vocal pride in their race), Negroes, the silent majority of persons of African heritage, and colored, persons of African descent who still accept the white stereotype of themselves.

of a mutual responsiveness such that every member in a group counseling session reacts immediately, spontaneously, and sympathetically to the sentiments and attitudes of every other member (Hinsie & Campbell, 1960). It is an attitudinal level of positiveness which should exist at the beginning of and throughout the relationship, whether dyadic or group.

Because of the current racial cataclysm in the American society, rapport is understandably strained between the white and the black. Black-black rapport may also be strained, if the counselee perceives the black counselor to be an "Uncle Tom," even if he is well-trained. It is important for the counselor, be he white or black, to realize that rapport can change from positive to negative and vice versa, even in the same interview.

Middle-class counselors must not be too quick to relegate their counseling responsibilities to sub-professionals, just because they consider themselves ostracized momentarily by the black counselee. If the individual perceives the counselor to be a genuine person, his initial reserve usually gives way to acceptance in due time. This aspect of the counseling relationship will be discussed more fully in the ensuing chapters.

Although Negroes are discussed as a group here, it is important to realize that not all black people are alike. The problems inherent in relating to various segments of black people are different. Establishing positive rapport with adolescents is quite different from what obtains either with young adults or adults. Males present problems uniquely different from those presented by females. In general, Southern Negroes are easier to relate to than those born and reared in the North; and as has already been suggested, there are differences between urban and rural Negroes. These, then, are some of the issues discussed in the chapters to come.

2

Counseling Negro Adolescents

With the advent of the Negro revolution, strained rapport between the black professional and blacks in general has lessened. For the most part, all black persons are potential soul brothers and treat each other as such. Only the obviously "white washed" are excluded from the brotherhood. Thus, in this chapter, the dynamics of the interpersonal relationship between the white counselor and the Negro counselee are analyzed. This is not to say that the black counselor may not have some of the same problems which the white counselor has in relating to Negroes; however, differences in color are perhaps more basic than differences in value orientation which may exist in the black-black counseling relationship.

Rogers (1958) has discussed the characteristics of a helping relationship, which should exist if the counselor is to be effective. In the case of the white counselor, it is not enough that he be able to give positive answers to the questions raised by Rogers, but he must also consider the possibility that his race may render him ineffectual in spite of his personality, theory, or other armamentaria. His race may be a debilitating strike against him even before he begins counseling suspicious Negro youths.

On first consideration, it may appear that the white counselor's race would be a decided advantage, in view of the historical reaction of Negroes to white professionals. The feeling that white doctors, dentists, lawyers, and other professionals are more competent than their own has been rather widespread among Negroes in this country. The white professional was looked upon, just because of his race, as being more able than the Negro counterpart, who was often distrusted and labelled pretender or charlatan by members of his own group. This stemmed from the "White is right" attitude which prevailed among Negroes.

However, this feeling does not exist for the counselor, because although often viewed in the same light as many other professionals (Patterson, 1958), he does not operate in the same manner as the latter. The extent to which he can be of service to his clients depends on his ability to establish rapport with them. The nature of the relationship will determine the client's willingness to accept him and the degree to which he will reveal himself in the interview. Self-disclosure, according to Jourard (1959), is a factor in the process of effective counseling and psychotherapy, and there is some evidence to suggest that Negroes are more reserved in this area than are whites (Jourard & Lasakow, 1958). When the factor of ethnic difference is added to self-disclosure reserve, the white counselor may be faced with almost insurmountable obstacles in the counseling relationship with Negro adolescents (Woods, 1958).

Sources of Potential Difficulties

Fibush (1965), Middleton (1963), Woods (1958), and Trent (1954) have suggested sources of potential difficulties which the white professional may encounter in counseling Negroes. The counselor may experience difficulty, first of all, because he is ignorant of his clients. He may think that because he has lived near and gone to school with Negroes that he knows them as a group, without ever considering that, historically, Negroes have been artists at deception. In order to stay in communication with whites, as they had to do to survive, black people approached them in a suppliant and inferior manner just to gain many favors which otherwise would not have been granted (Killian, 1964). Although today the group resorts less frequently to Uncle Tom techniques, Negroes have withdrawn, usually out of necessity rather than volition, more and more into isolation, either in black ghettos or black suburbias. They lead lives and hold values that are in the main unknown to most whites. Surrounding themselves with race secrets, they often ventilate their repressed anger, hatred, and anxiety by telling race jokes, in which whites are generally the butt.

Many, especially the lower class, communicate in gestures and jargon, which are unintelligible to the average white person. Consider "Member," "Shoe," "Brother," "Us," or "Boot" for Negro; "Ofay," "Honkie," "Grey," or "Paddie" for white; or "Soul food" or "Soul music" for food r music which is appreciated especially by blacks.

The fact that the Negro maintains an ethnic secretiveness indicates to some extent his feelings, covert or overt, toward whites. To him, whites are outsiders and as such are not to be trusted. The history of their behavior is against them. Negative feelings toward whites remain because "most whites," according to Arnold Rose (1949), "are still acting toward Negroes on the basis of old stereotypes, even when they have no deliberate or strong prejudices." Thus, it is important that white counselors examine their feelings toward blacks, for if they bring to the counseling interview personal bias against racial and ethnic minorities, these will intrude directly or indirectly upon their attempts to apply professional skills (Record, 1961). Even the counselor who does not bring to the interview biased feelings will find it necessary to examine himself carefully. He must be able to communicate his total personality to the client in an unambiguous manner. Just verbalizing what he is, is ineffectual, for a message is always transmitted with the stamp of the sender's total personality, not just a segment of it. In other words, what he is speaks so loudly that the counselee cannot hear what he says.

Moreover, it is not enough to understand himself and to purge himself of residual prejudices and preconceived racial ideas; he must also strive to understand his clients, even if they are hostile, angry, and suspicious. Clark (1963) has noted the alienation of Negro youngsters and their hatred for whites. Cothran (1951), in his study of 341 Negro adults, detected strong anti-white feelings in New Orleans. Milner (1953) has noted among Negroes a paranoid-like antipathy to "all whites." This antipathy does not allow the Negro to evaluate and react to them as individuals. These, then, are feelings which the white counselor needs to recognize, accept, and try to cope with, even before he can start to provide a helping relationship with such clients.

Background of the Student

The counselor cannot understand the feelings of the Negro student by observing him *in vacuo*. He must apprise himself of the whole psychosocial background out of which the student comes and into which his parents retreat for protection from ambiguous situations, insults, and possible humiliations. His knowledge of whites may be of little value to him. He needs to understand the value system embraced by the student's family; he should know how these values influence the child's attitude toward him as a counselor and toward the school as an institution, for values form a bridge between social structure and behavior (Kohn, 1963). The Negro mother's child-rearing objectives, based on her values, are apt to differ from those of most whites. Her most immediate and focal concern is meeting the physical needs of her children. She has little time and energy to concentrate on their educational and social needs. Further, the Negro, especially the lower-class, displays a pervasive passivity toward life's adversities (Woods, 1958). The condition of anomie to which all Negroes, particularly the male, are exposed (Sprey, 1962) and the economic impotence of the father (Goff, 1950) influence the child's total outlook on life. Undeniably, the Negro mother is the source of authority in a majority of black families (Dai, 1953). Therefore, the mother's concern and aspirations for her offspring are significantly more indicative of what the child is or may become than are the expressed concerns of the father (Bell, 1963). In general, the counselor must deal with the mother. Although the father may accompany her to a conference, it is the mother who usually does the talking. Attempts to get reactions from him are not very fruitful, even when he is present. Even if the father comes to the office unaccompanied, he is usually representing his wife, who could not be present.

The Negro Youth

Himes (1961) indicates that Negro teenage culture is conditioned by four decisive factors: race, inferiority, deprivation, and "youthfulness." Trent (1954), in investigating the influence of white and Negro experimenters, found that black kindergarten children were very much aware of race. They responded differently to white and Negro investigators when presented the same stimuli. This would suggest that kindergarten Negro children have not only become race conscious, but that they have also learned to be cautious when dealing with whites. Goff (1950) suggests that as black children mature, they acquire progressive sensitivity to race. She found that Negro children at ten and twelve years of age reacted intensely to subtle and overt discrimination and segregation. Thus, the white counselor must be aware of the built-in suspicion and fear of whites which black children bring to school with them.

The Negro student has been conditioned to feel that he is inferior and of little value. Such a self-concept is apt to influence his whole life. The fact that he is unable to accept himself, because of his race, may have direct bearing on the extent to which he can accept the counselor, for there is some evidence to suggest that the extent to which the individual accepts himself is directly related to his ability to accept others (Trent, 1957). The youngster's negative self-concept not only colors his relationship with others, but it also impedes the learning process as Landsman (1962) and Sarvis (1965) have indicated.

In addition to the debilitating results of poor self-concepts, boys are hampered by the psychological effects of their oppressive matriarchal home environment. Maturing males in female-dominated homes must either conform to what might be called "female patterns" or renounce the home and identify with the gang in the street (Thompson, 1962). In attempting to escape the feminizing influences of the Negro woman-dominated domain, they find the street an important social institution and a significant factor in their lives (Himes, 1961). Because of the woman's experiences with men whom she does not trust, she feels that her male children can fend for themselves. She thus releases them to the street at an early age and turns her attention to her girls, who receive much more succorance than do boys. As a result, black girls perceive themselves more highly accepted than the boys and intrinsically more valued by their parents (Ausubel, 1958). Black boys must declare their masculinity in the most direct way they know how. This often involves avoidance of women, whom they view as trying to emasculate them, scorn for middle-class standards, including striving for academic achievement, and hatred of authority (Thompson, 1962). They quickly assume the American masculine conviction that education and "culture" are feminine concerns and thus are not for them. Often, women teachers are looked upon as dehydrated, desexualized automatons, for whom they have either contempt or pity, depending on their individual bent. Men teachers are frequently suspected of being not quite "right," especially white men teachers, since black males, particularly the lower-class ones, perceive white men to be somewhat effeminate anyway.

The lower-class Negro adolescent attempts to project himself as being "bad," i.e., rough and tough. He spits through his teeth to denote defiance, strength, and power. He lifts and pulls on his scrotum in public, especially when in the company of his peers, to denote sexual prowess (i.e., power and strength); and, living from day to day, he postures an indifference to order and authority on every hand. In general, this behavior may be considered compensatory for personal devaluation.

In relating to the counselor, whom he views as an authority figure or "The Man," the black adolescent is apt to be hesitant, blatant, or both, not only because the counselor is different, "a square," but also because it is inconceivable to him that an outsider, a "Honkie," can "do anything" for him (Woods, 1958). The counselor can penetrate his rough exterior by showing some familiarity with, or at least a tolerance of, the influences motivating him. However, overnight magical changes in self-concept should not be expected.

On the other hand, the Negro girl does not present the same degree of challenge, probably because she is more self-accepting than the boy. The love and acceptance which she has received in the home make her more self-assured. Because she is more self-accepting and confident, she accepts other people more readily, as Tuma and Gustad suggest (1957). The counselor should find it considerably easier to establish rapport with the girl than with the boy.

It is important to recognize that many Negroes suffer from a series of problems in identification, stemming from cultural conflicts, caste restrictions, and minority status, mediated in part through family structure (Brody, 1961). The counselor must cope, as well as he can, with these problems; but his efficiency tends to be minimized if he allows himself to become a "bleeding heart." Above all, he should resist the temptation to slap the counselee on the back, while assuring him that everything will be all right. This, coming from a white person, is apt to be received with contempt, at least in the beginning of the relationship. With most Negroes, race and the resultant variety of problems it presents are serious matters, not to be taken lightly, especially by whites.

Although race has an isolating effect, Negroes react differently to their badge of color. There are distinct class differences. It is important to understand the dynamics and motivations of the black middle-class family. The fear of engendering or justifying social discrimination leads the middle-class Negro to improve his and his children's standards of personal conduct and morality, which are more stringent than the corresponding standards of middle-class whites (Karon, 1958, p. 35). Because of the rigidity of the home, children from black bourgeois families are often compulsive in their dress, their determination to achieve, and their desire to please. The counselor should have little difficulty establishing rapport with students from such homes, for they, like their parents, are seeking to hurdle the last barriers to full acceptance by whites. Many of these youngsters may become "clinging vines" to the white counselor, whose acceptance of them may imply that they are indeed fully accepted by whites in general.

The Counselor in Context

Even though the counselor may recognize many problems besetting Negro students, the social system in which he works prescribes to some extent his scope of operation. As Shertzer and Stone (1963) have pointed out, the expectations of his publics influence his behavior.

The counselor's Negro clients, either because of social conditioning or distrust of whites, may expect only information from him. Their tendency to doubt his interest in them is apt to be most pronounced, depending on the region of the country in which they live and its extent of urbanization. The counselor should accept reserve and reticence and not become a "jolly good fellow," for such behavior can confirm what the youngster may have suspected all along: "This 'Honkie' is playing me for a fool."

Parents

Contact with students is indirectly a contact with their parents, for youngsters are almost certain to mention that they have a white counselor. The middle-class parent may be flattered for the reasons already suggested. The lower-class parent may be suspicious; and the least misunderstanding on the part of the student is apt to bring Mother to school, even if Father is home, for it is the Negro woman who feels, as a result of her historical experience in working for and around whites, that she knows "how to handle white people." Thus, the counselor should not be alarmed if the mother storms into his office fit to fight. How he handles the initial contact with this type of parent may determine his effectiveness in future counseling with black youths.

Negro Co-workers

The counselor works with others, Negro and white. Undoubtedly, he will receive a great deal of advice on how to handle "those kids." If he is surrounded by a majority of black teachers, he may be inclined to accept the Negro co-worker's analysis of "the problem" as the last word, because he feels that Negroes should know what they are talking about, since they are Negroes. This is a tenuous assumption, for middle-class blacks share with whites many of the same attitudes toward and evaluations of lower-class Negroes, including, in certain cases, the attribution of blame to blacks themselves for their treatment by whites (MacIver & Page, 1949). It is not unusual to encounter black teachers who are more rigid in their evaluation of Negroes than are white teachers. Often they view the problem inherent in educating and counseling Negro students as stemming from the students' and their parents' laziness, indifference, and crassness.

White Co-workers

The counselor should also be objective in listening to the theories and understandings volunteered by white co-workers. Although many of them may be sincere in their desire to understand and help, they too are handicapped by the same lack of perception and appreciation of the problems facing Negroes as is the counselor himself. Even though the counselor should be open to suggestions, he must remember that *he* is the counselor. If he is dedicated to his job and wants to be effective in his role, he will have to do a great deal of homework in sociology and the psychology of race and race relations to understand how the Negro views his problems.

The Administration

The expectations of the school administration also affect the counselor's performance. The counseling service cannot function effectively in the absence of complete support from the school administrator. A major function of the high school principal is that of developing a willingness on the part of the whole faculty to accept and help youngsters to adjust to the integrated school environment. If students feel rejected in the classroom, the auditorium, the gymnasium, or the cafeteria, no amount of reassurance by the counselor will convince them that they are accepted. The principal, in the ultimate analysis, determines to a great extent how successful the counselor is in counseling black youngsters. His leadership or lack of it in the area of race relations impinges on the counselor's ability to carry out his assignment successfully.

The Community

The school is a subsystem of the total community, which determines how the high school functions to help its citizens. If the community expresses, either through language or deed, reservations toward its black students, the job of the principal and the counselor is made more difficult. If this should be the case, it is not enough that the principal and the counselor institute race relations programs in the school; but they should, if no one else does, educate the community in its responsibility for educating all the children of all the people.

The counselor, working in the counseling center, a subsystem of the institution, must function as best he can in the role to which he has been assigned. The problem of race difference need not be an insurmountable one, for when the counselee senses that the counselor is able, despite the obvious racial difference, to understand his special circumstances and problems and to identify with him in his struggles to meet his emotional and material needs, the counselee and the counselor can establish positive rapport on which many problems can be solved (Fibush, 1965).

In doing so, however, communication techniques are important. The counselor must be aware of his approach to communicating with the black student and his parents, for the student's attitude toward counseling and the counselor may be negative as has been suggested by Record (1961). He not only identifies the counselor with authority and discipline but also brings to any conference his own racial suspicions, backed by his own valid and painful experiences. The experiences which his parents and loved ones have communicated to him also support his own limited ones. Any communication *faux pas*, spoken or gestured, may destroy the relationship beyond repair.

The communication which the counselor undertakes with low-status black parents is apt to be strained and viewed with suspicion, not because of race alone, but because they view most communications, written or oral, as sources of trouble (Record, 1961). Their experiences with summonses, draft notices, and overdue bills, and their contacts with rent collectors and social caseworkers have taught them to be reserved, noncommittal, or afraid to participate in businesslike communication. Personal, direct, face-to-face contact with parents on a continuing basis is essential and instructive and should eventually allay their suspicions.

Guidelines for the Guidance of Negro Students

Trueblood (1960) offers guidelines for counselors of Negro students. They merit repeating here:

1. Organize the guidance program early.
2. Plan the guidance program to be individual and group, to include early opportunities to study occupations.
3. Advise about occupational and educational choice on the basis of national trends.
4. Learn as much as possible about the cultural and social background of the Negro.
5. Learn about the effects of discrimination and segregation on the personality development of the Negro student.
6. Recognize that the Negro student is apt to be deficient in reading skills.
7. Remember the important role of the parent of the Negro in the motivational factors related to the desire for additional educational and vocational success.
8. Counsel with the Negro in good faith concerning his educational and vocational opportunities.
9. Use tests with caution.
10. Use a variety of data in attempting to identify the capabilities of the Negro student: i.e., performance, aptitude, family occupational and educational background.

11. Learn about financial aid available for continuing education beyond high school.
12. Study talent search programs — components, steps, and minimum essentials.
13. Utilize community resources to help in the guidance of Negro students.

The counseling of Negro students presents more challenging problems than the counseling of white students, because of the factors of race, deprivation, and lack of academic skills prerequisite to success in schools which are geared in the main to meet the needs of middle-class white students. Thus, counseling ethnically different youngsters is not easy for anyone. When the factor of racial difference is added to the already existing variables, the white counselor may be presented with a more difficult task than he would have if he were counseling white students; even so, these obstacles are not insurmountable, if the counselor works in an environment in which all races are allowed to develop to their optimum.

3

Counseling Negro Students
for College

Counseling Negro students for college is one of the most challenging problems facing counselors and educators today. Already, many gains have been made in the field of civil rights, and others are forthcoming; however, the civil rights struggle will have been for naught, unless blacks are prepared to take advantage of new opportunities. Industry and business are seeking black applicants to fill a variety of positions, but it is evident that the number of qualified persons is limited.

In view of new opportunities now available, it appears that as one kind of discrimination disappears on the American scene, another is about to rear its head. That is, discrimination based on race is being replaced by discrimination based on class, and unfortunately the same people, the Negroes, are apt to suffer from the latter type if they are not prepared educationally to enjoy the fruits of equal opportunity.

In order to head off this possible catastrophe for Negroes, educators not only need to recognize and come to grips with the problems of educating and graduating black youths from secondary school, but they should be cognizant of the urgency of getting more minority students into college. For several generations the vicious cycle of the uneducated and undereducated has perpetuated itself in this country

(Swinehart, 1963). The trend must be scotched if Negroes are to move into the mainstream of the American society. It is not enough that minority youths be admitted to integrated public schools at the elementary and secondary levels. After graduating from high school, they must have equal opportunity to further their education. In this area, the high school counselor plays an important role.

Problems in College Counseling

The diverse problems inherent in college counseling are challenging and rewarding to solve. While the likelihood of helping a Negro college aspirant with a less than average academic record and little or no money is not good, once the way is found the counselor will feel that it was worth all the effort, when, four years later, he sees the once inarticulate, unsure, impoverished, gangling adolescent, now a man, marching with head high to receive his college diploma and, consequently, a better chance in life.

Parents play a significant role in a youngster's going to college. Herein lies a baffling problem in counseling for college. The parents' indifference, apathy, and ignorance may be disarming to the counselor who has been accustomed to counseling middle-class white parents about college plans for their children. Sending a son or daughter to college requires early planning. It means that the student must take college-oriented courses early in his school career. A youngster who has chosen the easy path will regret it four years later, especially if he should decide to attend college, for the likelihood of his getting admitted may be slight. As college enrollments soar, entrance requirements become more stringent. The counselor should encourage the Negro student to take college prep courses if it appears that he has the slightest chance of succeeding in the classes. The student should not be assigned as a matter of course to vocational and nonacademic curricula just because he is Negro. To do this is to seal his tomb for a better life in this country. Although many minority students, choosing to take the easy road, may wish to pursue nonacademic curricula, the counselor owes it to the student's parents and to his country to vigorously counsel him about the realities of the future; i.e., let him know that he will be handicapped occupationally without a college education. Because of racial discrimination, a college education is more important to Negroes than it is to whites.

Many Negro parents, although optimistic about their children's future, fail to make long range plans to assure them better lives than they themselves had. While they often sacrifice to buy television sets, expensive automobiles, and other material things, they are reluctant to deny themselves in the same way to help further their offspring's education. First, the counselor should help such parents to understand the value of higher education for their children. Secondly, he should illustrate to them that sending a child through college is very much like paying for a car. Most colleges have pay-as-you-go plans. Parents can be shown that undergraduate college payments may extend over a four year period, that car payments usually extend over a three year period, and that the results from a college education will afford the student extra dividends for the rest of his life.

In some cases, it may be necessary to encourage parents to borrow money. Most larger banks have college loan plans whereby the bank pays the student's college bills while parents make monthly payments to the bank. Lower-class parents are generally reluctant to borrow. The counselor should help them understand the value and procedure for borrowing. Banks often have brochures which explain their college loan plans. It is advisable to invite a bank representative to speak to the PTA. By so doing, all parents, not just senior class parents, will benefit from whatever information is presented. This technique is recommended in order to get parents to start thinking as early as possible about ways to finance a college education. A bank representative should be invited to appear before the PTA at least once a year. A similar approach may be used in explaining the National Defense Loan plan which is administered through colleges.

Another problem often encountered by counselors when counseling for college with lower-status Negro parents is their apparent indifference to or fear of education. They may feel that since they did not go to college and "did all right" that their children can do the same. This attitude is especially prevalent in regard to their male children. If anyone goes to college out of the family, it is apt to be the girls — not the boys, who are often kept home to help "keep the family going." Today about two-thirds of all Negro college students are women — just the reverse of the white college population. The situation is a challenge to the counselor. First, he must start early — at least in the 9th grade — to encourage parents to include a college education in their hopes and aspirations for their children. Secondly, he should encourage them to send their sons as well as their daughters to college, for the future of blacks in this country depends on the Negro man's being able to meet the masculine responsibility in society. Unless he is able to do this, the vicious matriarchal cycle and the economic impotence of the black male are apt to continue indefinitely.

The counselor is also faced with the reluctance of the student to commit himself to the possibility of his going to college. The student may indicate that he intends to go to college eventually, but that he is unable to go right away or that he will work a year and then go, or that he does not think that he can do college work. He refuses to commit himself to the idea of going to college, because he fears that there is no need to build up high hopes, since he will not be able to go anyway. The counselor needs to help the counselee gain insight into the advantages of going to college immediately after graduation. The longer he stays out of college, the more he will become committed to other goals. Often, in the case of the male adolescent, the alternate goal is the army; with the girl, it is likely to be marriage. Unless the student's record is extremely poor, he should be encouraged to try *some* college. Negro boys, because of the fear of achieving (i.e., academic achievement is often viewed as being effeminate, especially in all-black schools), generally do not do well in high school, a fact which is not always predictive of college potential and success. Black boys should be counseled toward college or at least some type of advanced training, because increasingly included among the unemployed today are individuals who have graduated from high school. Kalish (1966) indicates that the median educational attainment of the unemployed four years ago was ten years. One-third of the unemployed sample had finished high school. These, in the main, were young black males.

Negro students also display an apparent apathy in matters pertaining to their being admitted to college. They are reluctant to write to the admissions office at the college of their choice to obtain application forms. Even when the forms arrive, many are not prompt in completing and returning them. They show the same lack of concern about writing to their chosen colleges to ask about scholarship aid, loans, or work on campus. The counselor should not be dismayed at what seems to be apathy and indifference on the part of lower-class black youth. They are often unacquainted with or even fearful of formal communication (Record, 1961). Their experiences have been with "bad news": a summons, a draft notice, an overdue bill, or a telegram announcing the death of a relative. The counselor can assist students with college communication by making up a dummy letter to a college, asking for an application for admission, scholarship aid, and other such information. When there is a large number of students who show the same lack of formal communication skills, it saves time to meet with them in groups, in order to give them information and direction about communicating with colleges.

Once students have received the requested forms and information from their chosen colleges, they should be encouraged to see the counselor to ask questions about anything related to filling out forms. The counselor needs to be aggressive in this area. Instead of waiting for students to come to him with questions, he should send for them in order to determine the progress they are making toward getting admitted to college. It is helpful to keep a college admissions progress check sheet on students, as illustrated in the table below.

The check sheet contains spaces for listing several students' names and for checking opposite each the progress or steps completed in getting admitted to college. The form may also include the names of the colleges to which the student has applied, the date of each application, the status of each application, and other information desired. The essential point here is that the counselor be aware of the progress of each student. In this way, he can send for students to keep check on them and to ascertain whether they are going to meet college admissions deadlines.

A sixth recurring problem which the high school college counselor encounters in counseling black students, especially those from low-status families, is their failure to follow through on college entrance examination procedures. Nearly every college in the country requires that the applicant take an entrance examination. The two most widely used instruments are the Scholastic Aptitude Test (SAT), administered by the College Entrance Examination Board, and the American College Test (ACT), administered by the American College Testing Program. Secondary school administrators and counselors receive announcements during late spring or early fall indicating the dates and procedures for taking the college admissions examinations. Black students frequently need intensive counseling to motivate them to take the tests. It is important that counselees understand that final decisions on their application for admission to college cannot be made until they have taken one of the required exams.

The college counselor should screen seniors who indicate some ability for college and consult with them about taking the external tests. Since students are often uncertain about how to complete applications

College Application Check Sheet

Name of Student	Letter of application mailed	Application received	Application returned	Admission granted
1. John Doe	x	x		
2. Mary Jones	x			
3. George Hayes				
4. James Smith	x	x	x	x
5. Susan Scott	x			

for taking tests, the counselor needs to assist them in this area. It is suggested that a sample form be completed and placed in a conspicuous place so that students may see how applications for taking the SAT or the ACT are to be filled out.

That many students who apply to take the above mentioned tests never take them for various reasons may also surprise the college counselor. On the morning of the test, they either oversleep or stay home to run errands for the family. The counselor needs to stress the importance of taking external tests. In some cases it may be necessary for the school to furnish a car pool or to provide a bus to make sure all youngsters get to the test center on time. Although this may seem like coddling, it must be realized that people who have had few experiences involving appointments and other formalities are often unaware of the significance of punctuality.

It is generally recognized that youngsters from low socio-economic homes do not feel the need for achievement that those from middle-class homes experience. Although there appears to be little the counselor can do to increase achievement need, since it is internally structured, it is suggested that individual counseling be continuous in order to help students internalize strong motivational patterns. Unless something is done in this direction, students are apt to be indifferent not only during the time they are taking the tests, but they also are apt to be apathetic to the low test scores which they make on the tests and assume an "I-told-you-so" attitude.

The seventh problem inherent in counseling black students for college is their tendency to get "cold feet" during summer months and decide not to go to college after all. During the school year they may remain interested in going to college because the counselor continues to reinforce their decision. However, when school is out, pre-college anxiety may set in. They become anxious about the new environment ahead, the adequacy of their clothes for campus life, or their ability to do college work. It is therefore advisable that the high school, whenever possible, provide a year-round college counselor. Someone should be available for consultation during the summer. Students may receive communications from colleges which they do not understand. Parents are frequently unable to aid in interpreting such correspondence. Thus, the college counselor should be on duty at the school to aid in last minute dilemmas.

The problems discussed may differ from one school or community to another. Certainly, socio-economic differences are significant factors. Middle-class youngsters who are blessed with interested parents present fewer and less nodal problems than lower-class students, whose parents have marginal education. Black and white bourgeois students are enough alike that if the counselor knows how to counsel one group, he should be able to counsel the other; or, at least, this should prevail in most cases.

Aggressive Counseling

Although the counselor may be theoretically opposed to the idea, it may be necessary for him to engage in aggressive counseling with the Negro student. Lefcourt (1963) concludes that the Negro problem is similar in some ways to what has been called the "psychology of poverty." Economically deprived persons who commonly have few successful experiences tend to develop fatalistic, externally controlled perceptions. These perceptions, in turn, may overly determine further failures by increasing failure-avoidant and defensive behavior. Add to this fact the inherent anti-intellectualism pervasive in the lower class in general (Riessman, 1965), and the counselor is faced with a difficult task in persuading parents and students that college is imperative.

Parents and their children often accept whatever comes in life. They cannot see why one should get all bothered about things anyway or may feel that "The Lord will provide." The counselor should be resolute with such parents. He needs to help them see the need for a college education. If they come to the PTA meetings, reluctant parents should be placed in discussion groups with parents who already have children in college — which will provide an opportunity for them to ask questions about how it feels to have a son or daughter in college. Afterwards, the counselor may follow up such meetings with calls or visits to discuss further the idea of college for the boy or girl.

Once the interest is developed, parents need to know how to finance a college education. The counselor can be a careful guide here. He may help them fill out Parent Confidential Statements (PCS) or other such papers; but whatever is necessary, he should be available to help. Low-status parents are sometimes hesitant to ask for help or advice. They may feel that asking questions will make them look ignorant. Thus, rather than *look* ignorant, they will remain uninformed about something which may be very important. The counselor needs to be aggressive and not wait for parents to ask questions. He must encourage them to follow through on requirements and procedures necessary for admission to college. Even after the students are in college, the counselor should telephone parents periodically, especially during the first semester that students are in college, to inquire about the students' progress and to offer assistance if problems exist, financial or otherwise.

It is not enough that the counselor aggressively counsel parents; he must also counsel the students. They must see the need for college — they must be shown how they can do it. That is, if they feel that they can do college work, but that money is the great deterrent, the counselor should indicate the array of avenues open to them for financing a college education. This assumes, of course, that the counselor himself is informed.

Even if financial resources are available, students may still need confidence that they can actually do college work. There are at least three ways to help them overcome self-doubt. First, the counselor may take them to the college of their choice and let them mix freely with students there. Hopefully, they will learn that in many ways college is very much like high school. Secondly, the school may arrange for college students to visit the high school attended by black students, in order that college and high school students may mingle and get to know each other. This should eventuate in the black students' realizing that college students are pretty much the same as they. Thirdly, the high school may choose to have college-high school social events. College students may be invited to senior dances. This would provide opportunity for the students to mix informally and may often result in the high school students' getting invited to visit nearby colleges.

The point is that counselors must not wait for lower-status Negro students to come to them for assistance. They should whet an interest in and desire for college. If they do some of the things suggested in this passage, they are engaging in aggressive counseling.

College Admissions Representatives

The college admissions counselor and the high school college counselor need to work together, if success is to be realized in counseling Negro students for college. The inexperienced college admissions counselor needs help in understanding the background of black students. While his youth is undoubtedly an asset in counseling high school students, his lack of understanding of the significance and meaning of test scores and other information as these relate to the college potential of Negro students is a handicap. Further, a lack of understanding or appreciation of Negroes limits the extent to which he can work effectively with them.

The high school counselor needs to help the college representative become more knowledgeable about Negroes and their potential, which is often not reflected in test scores. The counselor may indicate to the college representative where previous black graduates have matriculated and point out their college success. He should show the admissions counselor the kinds of test scores these students had and indicate that, in spite of their marginal scores, they are succeeding in college.

Further, the high school counselor needs to attend High School-College Conferences and share with college officials what information he has on Negro students, their needs, difficulties, and aspirations. This can be extremely helpful, for college recruiters are often handicapped by lack of information on and fear of recruiting black students. College financial-aid officers must be convinced that in spite of the apparent marginal status of the Negro student, he is worthy of consideration for financial assistance.

College representatives need to understand the trilogy of problems facing Negro students seeking college admission. First, there is the perennial problem of getting admitted. The modest high school record, as already suggested, is often not reflective of college potential. Even if admissions officials concede this point, they or their financial-aid officers are often reluctant to grant financial aid. However, if financial aid is denied, admitting black students beset by great monetary needs would do little good, for few would be able to remain to graduate. Moreover, the problem of admission and financial aid is complicated by still another — the student's need for adjustive counseling once he is in college. The *Instant Negro* on campus will need help in adjusting to the strangeness of his new environment, especially if he goes to a predominantly white college, and the lack of a strong need for achievement will hamper his progress unless there is someone there who shows an interest in his welfare.

The Predominately Negro or Interracial College

Helping the student and his parents decide on what kind of college they should select is a problem which the counselor ultimately faces. Black students and their parents are often in a dilemma deciding for or against a predominately Negro college.

The Negro College

In this country there are 116 colleges and universities established and operated primarily for Negroes (Wright, 1960). In general, they are located in Southern and border states. Seventy-one are private and forty-five are tax-supported. Of the nearly 200,000 undergraduate black students enrolled in college, slightly over two-thirds are in these institutions. Jerome Holland (1965), former president of Hampton

Institute, explains that many Negroes desire to attend a Negro college so they can acquire life-long friends and participate without restrictions in extra-curricular activities, especially in Negro Greek letter organizations.

The majority of Negro teachers in this country completed their undergraduate work at Negro colleges. Since they remember with fondness their college days, they are inclined to counsel Negro students to attend one of these colleges too. It is for this reason that a Negro college may be the black counselor's first thought when counseling Negro students. The teacher and the counselor alike frequently express concern that the student would not be happy or would not achieve were he to go to an interracial college. Cost is also a prohibitive factor. In general, it costs considerably less to attend a Negro college than an interracial institution. These, then, are some of the reasons why the majority of black students continue to choose Negro colleges.

An equal education is the key to true equality in other areas of life. On the American scene, the predominately Negro college is still considered a segregated institution (Holland, 1964). If it is agreed that students should be permitted to grow and learn in an integrated environment, then it seems necessary to break the Negro college tradition among Negroes. Although most of these colleges now have an integrated faculty and a few white students, they are still considered segregated institutions and are therefore less desirable for preparing students to live in an integrated society than are interracial institutions.

In all fairness and objectivity, the only adequate generalization one can make about Negro colleges is that they are uniformly worse than their white counterparts. First, their students are almost exclusively black, a fact that would not necessarily make for a weak college were all other things equal. Most black students come from poor all-Negro high schools which have suffered for so long the pangs of discrimination and *de facto* segregation. Black colleges have been forced to take the students "where they are." While, in general, Southern education for both Negroes and whites is inferior to its Northern counterpart, it is far worse for blacks than for whites (Karon, 1958). The cumulative effects of an inferior elementary and secondary education have been reflected in the type of student who enters and graduates from the Negro college (Frazier, 1960). The Negro college student is generally bankrupt in verbal skills. On national examinations he has generally scored extremely low when compared with white collegians. The disparity stems in the main from the vicious cycle of poorly prepared black college graduates teaching academically weak high school students who go on to struggling Negro colleges (Wright, 1960).

Interracial Colleges

In the past, few black students have sought admission to interracial or all-white colleges and universities. In many cases, the cost of attending was prohibitive. Also, students felt that their educational backgrounds were weak; they did not wish to appear academically dull in front of whites. Some black students, having grown up in segregated communities and having attended all-Negro high schools, either in the South or a Northern ghetto, felt uncertain and anxious around whites. However, today, there are good reasons to believe that such fears are dissipating.

For nearly twenty years the National Scholarship and Service Fund for Negro Students has assisted more than 20,000 Negro students to enroll in interracial colleges throughout the country. A few years ago, Clark and Plotkin (1963), under the sponsorship of NSSFNS, made an extensive study of the success of these students. Of the 1,519 collegians included in the study, they found that the net dropout rate was one-fourth the national average. Fewer than ten percent of the Negroes as compared to approximately 40 percent of white students did not complete college.

The study indicated further that black students enrolled in predominately white institutions of higher learning did average or better academic work. Thirty-one percent achieved an average of "B—" or better for the four years enrolled. Slightly less than ten percent graduated with honors and about one percent were elected to Phi Beta Kappa.

Sources of Assistance for Negro Students

There are two organizations which are geared especially to helping black students get into college and stay there. They are the National Scholarship Service and Fund for Negro Students (NSSFNS) and the National Achievement Scholarship Program for Outstanding Negro Students. NSSFNS is a non-profit, non-fee charging agency which in the past twenty years has helped over 20,000 black students gain admission to and secure some $18,000,000 in financial aid from over 500 interracial colleges and from NSSFNS itself.

The National Achievement Scholarship Program for Outstanding Negro Students seeks to identify, honor, and encourage superior academic attainment among Negro students. Four-year scholarships were awarded to more than 200 students in 1965–66, the Program's second year. Each scholarship was worth at least $1,000 over four years and could be increased according to need to as much as $6,000. In the spring of each year, secondary school officials nominate candidates from their junior classes for the scholarships.

There are, of course, other sources for assisting black students in realizing their college aspirations. The interested counselor should write to the organizations mentioned above. They will be able to furnish up-to-date information on scholarship sources. Addresses for the organizations are NSSFNS, 6 East 82nd Street, New York; and The National Achievement Scholarship Program, 990 Grove Street, Evanston, Illinois.

Further, the high school counselor is advised to write to colleges and universities throughout the country to find out if they have scholarships especially earmarked for black students. Many of them do, but do not advertise it for various reasons.

4

Counseling Black
College Students

Throughout the country, college campuses have become caldrons of racial unrest, reflecting in miniature the black and white disharmony evident in the society at large. On predominately white campuses black students have taken over campus buildings, demanded educational "relevance," and have sequestered themselves in dormitories, study nooks, and classes. College officials have been dismayed and perplexed at this chain of events. For the last few years, they have made special efforts to recruit more black students to their campuses; they have sought special stipends for them.

Faced with general campus unrest and stringent demands of black students, white college officials have pursued a containment policy in the attempt to keep down or curb campus violence. In general, they have given little attention to the far-reaching implications of their concessions to the hastily written demands.

Predominately black campuses have also had their share of student disquietude. Although the behavior of students on black and white campuses is very much alike, the motivation and goals are quite different. On white campuses, students have attacked the "racist" educational system head-on; on black campuses they have attacked it too, but more indirectly. Forced to attack their bourgeois soul brothers, whom they perceive as caretakers for "The Man," students have often found these indirect attacks more frustrating than their assaults on white social systems. White officials act for themselves; black officials in state supported and private institutions depend on the benevolence of "good" whites to keep their doors open. This undoubtedly helps to explain why unrest on black campuses has been more nodal than that in white colleges. In either case, however, students have sought "relevance." Student personnel workers have found themselves in the midst of the unrest.

Problems of Black College Students

Today, young people, both white and black, have a series of moral and philosophical problems which they struggle to resolve in their own minds. The war, racial conflict, pollution, and the growing impersonality in urban America are only a few of the perplexities disturbing college-age students. In addition, they are faced with the perennial problems of growing up: developing sexual polarity, achieving emotional and economic independence from parents and others, choosing and preparing for an occupation, and developing a philosophy of life. Black students, because of the status of their parents and forebears, experience a multiplicity of unique and almost insoluble problems which generally do not encumber their white counterparts, at least not to the same degree.

Impaired Self-concept

A general problem besetting black college students is low self-esteem, which emanates from childhood. The Negro child inherits an inferior caste status and almost inevitably acquires the negative self-concept that is a realistic ego reflection of such status (Ausubel & Ausubel, 1963). Through personal slights, blocked opportunities, and unpleasant contacts with whites and with institutionalized symbols of caste inferiority (segregated schools, neighborhood, and amusement areas) and more indirectly through mass media and the reactions of his own family, he gradually becomes aware of the social significance of racial membership.

Awareness of and knowledge about oneself are heavily influenced by social interaction, as White (1948) points out. The black child builds up his sense of self out of the responses made to him by others; through their acts and attitudes he learns how they perceive him and is influenced to perceive himself accordingly. Although Negro children definitely exhibit more negative self-evaluations than do white children (Keller, 1963), black girls tend to score higher on self acceptance than do boys (Berger, 1952). This can probably be explained to some degree historically. In general, black women have received wider acceptance by whites than black men. Since the Negro's ego structure is largely a reflection of the actual and legal status he enjoys in culture (Ausubel & Ausubel, 1963), it is understandable that black women have a more positive self-concept than do black men.

Although the "Black is beautiful" rhetoric is articulated by most black college students, it is doubtful that any significant modifications have taken place in the ego structure of black people in this country. The black rhetoric, chauvinistic dress, and other ethnic behavior may be characterized as reaction formation, not necessarily an indication of black pride. The individual who is psychologically secure has little need to scream out what he is. This is not to say that the current black protest is not healthy, both for Negroes and society itself. However, until whites accept blacks as equals, Negroes will undoubtedly continue to protest that they are just as good as the next person. They can hardly be secure in their blackness, so long as there is a need to protest their goodness.

Parental Dissociation

Developing a wholesome independence of parents and other adults is an important developmental task of adolescence (Havighurst, 1953). This task is prolonged and difficult for college students who depend on their parents for support. On the one hand, young people are self-reliant in terms of being able to make some of their own decisions for the first time; on the other, they are still dependent financially on their parents. Being able to make decisions without the wherewithal to implement them often leaves them frustrated, especially if their parents are not supportive of their courses of action. It is understandable that the relationship between college students and their parents is frequently tacitly strained.

There is reason to believe that black college students are more estranged from their parents than are white collegians. The middle-class black student is faced with difficult questions which he must answer. Should he, as a middle-class Negro, continue to try to make inroads into the mainstream of American society as his parents have done or should he join the camp which supports some form of separatism (Phillips, 1968)? Should he remain silent as the obviously racist society sits by and the gap between himself and the lowest-class black widens?

Black bourgeois parents are proud to see their sons and daughters go off to college. Although they want them to get a good education, they also expect them to get into the "social swing of things." This includes, among other things, becoming members of black Greek letter organizations. When they discover that their children are not interested in pledging, in attending the big ball of the season, or in the many other "must" social events, and that they instead let their hair go, they are dismayed, to say the least. At the same time, the students start to assess the goals and values of Mom and Pop. They find it difficult to either understand or accept the set of shifting attitudes about Negro-white relations which apparently their parents embrace. On the one hand, they say they are for integration; on the other, as Greek-letter, middle-class Negroes, they give all-black parties and attend all-Negro fraternity and sorority balls. Many middle-class black students are repelled by the thought that one day they may be just like their parents. Some, to the chagrin of their fathers and mothers, give up the middle-class "rat race" and leave college in the name of relevance.

Lower-class parents struggle to put their sons and daughters through college. In the main, they are people of "colored" mentality, who are not caught up in the "Movement." In many cases, they take their values and directions from their white employers, who often assist directly to help them finance their offspring's education. Such parents find it hard to understand what is happening to black students on college campuses. Although some lower-class black students try to convert their parents to "blackness," others simply give up and break off with them altogether. Their dissociation often starts with shorter and less frequent letters (except to ask for money) and fewer visits back home. Differences of opinion on the race question are not the only reason for dissociation. With lower-class parents, students frequently break off out of shame, not necessarily because Mother and Dad do not understand. It is an unconscious way of denying their past, a past of great deprivation, a past of which they are not proud, and a past of which their parents are a crucial part. In general, there seems to be a greater tendency for men to dissociate more readily and sooner than women. This can probably be explained in terms of the young man's struggle to break loose from the black matriarchy.

Drug Use

Recent reports indicate that college students are experimenting with a variety of drugs. How widespread the trend is, is up to conjecture, for the type, size, and location of the college undoubtedly determine the behavior of the student body. Although there is hardly consensus on why individuals use drugs, it is suspected that, in the case of black people, their pathological environment contributes to information about and use of narcotizing agents. Whereas white students may use drugs for kicks or the novelty, blacks may extend drug use as a way of life into the college environment.

Over 70 percent of all black people in this country live in urban areas characterized by blight, poverty, unemployment, and hustling. Adults without jobs and hope for the future escape the misery of the ghetto through the use of a variety of drugs. Often, they indoctrinate adolescents, especially males, into the same way of life at an early age. The junkie and the pusher are no strangers to youngsters from the ghetto. If they have not experimented with drugs before going to college, at least one of their relatives or friends has.

Early exposure to drugs and drug use may have positive or negative effects on student behavior. If the individual is determined to "make it" out of the ghetto, he may safely resist the temptation to experiment on the campus, for he knows firsthand the terrible toll drugs can exact. If, however, he perceives the use of drugs to be an indication or salvation of his manhood, he may want to use them, especially when in the company of friends, to prove his masculinity. Masculine protest and impaired self-concept seem to be significant reasons why black males use narcotizing agents in the American society.

This discussion of drug use among black collegians is not to suggest that all black students "smoke" or "shoot." Youngsters, middle- or lower-class, who have had a warm, wholesome relationship with their parents usually have little need to use drugs or even to experiment with them.

Loneliness

The black student on an integrated campus is apt to be lonely and perpetually homesick for the familiar. He misses the "happenings in Soulsville." This includes rapping with the gang, dancing to the sounds of soul music, and in general, the total stimulation of being around people who think, act, and feel as he does. The environment of the typical white campus is sterile and somehow false and unreal to him. White collegians talk about things that "don't matter" and do many things which are irrelevant to his life. This may help to explain why black students demand separate dormitories, dining rooms, and study nooks. Even a small number of blacks helps to recreate a part of "Soulsville" in an otherwise foreign environment. In effect, the black student experiences bi-cultural confusion on many predominately white campuses.

Academic Frustration

In recent years, white colleges and universities have launched intensive Negro recruitment programs. Although select institutions have implemented remedial procedures to help black students make a smooth transition from all-black high schools to almost all-white college environments, others have simply brought students on campus, hoping that they could or would adjust on their own. In general, students have met with academic success in colleges that have provided special tutoring, individualized plans, and intensive individual and group counseling for them. While some Negro students are well equipped to take a full academic load their first semester on campus, others should take a maximum of six or nine hours. Individualizing student programs is hardly possible on campuses where the student is required to take twelve or fifteen hours in order to be considered a full-time student or to live in the dormitory as a boarding student.

Student-Faculty Relations

Closely related to academic frustration is the problem of student-faculty relations. Many black students come from small high schools, staffed by dedicated teachers, the majority of whom are themselves black. Teachers, administrators, and counselors maintain close relations with students and their families, in an effort to help them remediate their educational disadvantage. The continuous support and encouragement of the students provide them with the incentive to study against many odds. Often, teachers literally beg students to learn. On many campuses students find that they, like their white counterparts, are only numbers. They seldom get to see their professors outside class or to get to know them as persons. Often, they get the impression that even though the recruiter expressed an interest in their coming to X College, the professors apparently do not share his concern.

Identity Crisis

In every society the individual must have a definite sense of identity. Who am I? What am I? These are important questions to which the Negro has yet to find answers. His forebears were uprooted over 300 years ago from their native Africa and subjected to the most deplorable human condition ever known in the history of mankind. Stripped of his culture, language, and religion — all those things which give men pride in their heritage — in this country the Negro has been a man in search of a past. Although his cultural heritage is somewhere lost in the slavocracy of the South, he rejects this past and reaches across the continent to Africa, which, unfortunately, is today a place foreign to him. Thus, the black man in this country is in a heritage limbo.

Indicative of the heritage void is the awful confusion about what he should be called: Negro, black, colored, or Afro-American. Although legal citizens of the United States, young blacks tend to identify with people on another continent, because their experiences in this country have been too horrific. Even though they declare themselves to be "black and beautiful," one gets the impression that their ethnic rhetoric is a terrible cry for identity, that their "I'm black and I'm proud" shouts are but the reaction formation of a people in search of an identity.

Not only is the black collegian tormented by the lack of racial identity, but he is also struggling to acquire his manhood. Whereas the white man regards his manhood as a birthright, the black male is fighting a constant battle to possess his (Grier & Cobbs, 1968). In the American society, his forebears have always held back for fear that they would be branded a "bad nigger." Their *maschismo* has been suppressed and denied. Unable to get and hold jobs in order to support his family, the black man has been forced to absent himself from the home, so that his wife and family could receive welfare checks.

The matriarchy is especially stifling to the developing male. He is forced to either submit to the woman's authority or reject it at an early age and take to the streets in search of manhood. In general, the black mother is supportive of her daughters, whom she wants to get an education, so they can look out for themselves, if necessary. She may also encourage her sons to complete high school and go to college, provided they are not too much like her "no-good husband." The lack of a male figure with whom to identify and the strong support of the mother mean that many black boys grow up very doubtful of their masculinity.

The absence of a father figure in the home also has telling effects on maturing females. Denied direct exposure to the male role in the family environment, young females grow up without a clear perception of their roles as housewives and mothers. Patterning themselves after their mothers, black females leave college with a degree, but with little likelihood of establishing a permanent and wholesome relationship with a spouse.

Compulsive Behavior

Upper- and middle-class Negroes, anxious to combat the Negro stereotype, live and act in a way which they feel would be approved by whites (Vontress, 1966). Many of them feel that black people bring social exclusion on themselves, because of their low morals and vulgar behavior. In order to counteract the black image, they often live stylized and constricted lives, especially when in the presence of whites. Middle-class parents, in an effort to bridge the last barriers to Negro acceptance in American society, demand strictness in speech, dress, and behavior of their children.

This may help to explain why students from black bourgeois families seem to lack spontaneity in much of their behavior. Instead of the usual Negro language of the ghetto, they often speak with an almost ersatz brogue. Unlike the abandonment expressed in the movements of the ghetto, their dance is apt to be tight and constrained. Their dress is often impeccable. In essence, their general behavior may be characterized as a denial of the Negro stereotype. In so deporting themselves, black, middle-class collegians generally appear more mature than their white counterparts.

Ambivalence Toward Whites

Although there is much discussion today about black militants who are reputedly anti-white, there is little real evidence to indicate that black people dislike dominant group members any more today than at other periods in the history of this country. Blacks and whites are currently more vocal in expressing their attitudes toward each other than previously. What appear to be anti-white feelings are undoubtedly a reaction to white rejection of black people. During the Negro's presence in this country, he has been seeking acceptance by people who deny his equality. If some blacks express either by their behavior or rhetoric that they hate whites, it should be understandable. However, what passes as hatred can be better characterized as ambivalence, at least on white college campuses.

If indeed blacks hated whites, they probably would not choose to enroll in predominately white colleges and universities. Generally, black students on white campuses want to be accepted. Their exclusiveness is an expression of fear of rejection, not hatred. Black and white confrontation sessions and encounter groups indicate this fact rather conclusively.

The Counselor

Who should he be? Should there be black counselors on predominately white campuses to service black collegians? What about white counselors in predominately black colleges? These are some of the questions frequently posed by college administrators and black students alike.

A well-trained counselor should be able to function in any environment. "Well-trained" means that the counselor is not only trained in the academics of his trade, but that he is also a sensitive, understanding, and accepting human being who continues to take stock of himself. Those around him sense his sincerity, honesty, and acceptance of others. The color of his skin, like a bald head, may constitute a temporary barrier, but once the counselee senses his genuine interest in him and his ability to help, initial reserve usually gives way to acceptance.

Well-trained counselors are few in number. College officials would be well advised to employ the best they can find. A poorly trained black counselor should not be employed simply because he is black, for once he has established rapport with his Negro clients, he renders them a disservice if he has nothing to offer but his blackness.

The Counselor's Role

The counselor can play a vital role not only in restoring peace and tranquility to college campuses, both black and white, but also in helping black students to resolve many of the problems distracting them from their academic pursuits. In fulfilling this role, he should be allegiant to the students, no matter what their cause or gripe may be. Instead of being perceived as an extension of the administration, he should be accepted by the collegians as one of them. An individual who is privy to the thoughts, feelings, and attitudes of black students, he is a roving counselor who mingles more with students on the campus than he does with the administration.

In order that counselors assume such a role, the administration must be secure; the administration must believe in the counselors they employ. Counselors should not be perceived as roving spies for college officials. Instead, they should be considered student advocates. When there are grievances to be articulated, the counselor should be there with students to help them verbalize complaints to the administration, without fear of losing his job.

The counselor should be able to play this role, be he white or black. Having a black professional on campus is not necessarily the answer. If he is perceived as "nigger in residence," he is more of a bane than boon to the administration and to the students. If on the other hand a black counselor stands up for the students, he undoubtedly will be looked up to as somebody who has "clout" and who is not afraid of white people. Again, this takes fortitude on the part of the administration to maintain in employment an individual who sides with students, especially student dissenters. However, a secure administration should be ready to do just this, if indeed it wants to bridge the generation gap.

Black Studies

In the last few years, black students have demanded curriculum relevance on college campuses. Their most vocal insistence has been for "Black Studies." Although there is hardly consensus as to what is meant by the phrase, it usually suggests an academic program of instruction designed to teach blacks about their heritage, the contributions of black people in the American setting, and in general, the human condition of Negroes in the United States. On many campuses, especially predominately white ones, black students have demanded the creation of Black Studies departments, the employment of black professors, and in some cases, all black classes.

The last demand — that white students be barred from the Black Studies classes — has created a great deal of controversy. The students maintain that the presence of whites creates what may be called a "staging effect." This implies that black students cannot be themselves when white collegians are around, that blacks behave as if "company" were present, and that whites are too retarded in their understanding of blacks to study the black heritage in the same classes with them. The administration insists that college classes must be open to all students, that if race relations are to be improved in this country, whites must be exposed to black studies, and that to deny them is to practice discrimination in reverse. The controversy continues.

Counselors who understand the plea of black students are needed urgently to resolve the current stand-off. In general, Negro students are demanding the rectification of history, the recognition of blacks as a part of the American scene, and an acknowledgement of their contribution to its culture. Seeing no hope in realizing this goal, they have asked for the extreme — Black Studies. If all college courses were revised to include relevant information about black people, Black Studies as an issue would probably not exist. However, instead of working toward such a goal, many college administrators have immediately capitulated to the demands of black students without understanding the motivation of their requirements. In so doing, they have unwittingly recreated in miniature the segregated society which is an anathema to the ideals of Americans devoted to equality.

The Negro College Environment

The counselor on a predominately black campus may find his job more difficult than it would be on a white campus. The Negro college, as a black social system, is infected with self-hatred, which is a basic personality component of most Americans of African descent (Vontress, 1966). Thus, black professors, administrators, and students have more difficulty relating harmoniously with each other than is the case with whites. Although a generation gap exists in the country as a whole, there is a wider ideological chasm between old and young Negroes than between their white counterparts, because young black people hate older blacks as they hate themselves. This is especially true in the case of collegians who identify with the ghetto and conservative professors who would preserve the system.

The counselor working in such an environment finds himself in a very sensitive and often vulnerable position. The black administrator considers himself accountable for the behavior of all his faculty, staff, and students. He demands complete allegiance from everyone, including the counselor. Instead of acting as student advocate, the counselor may be required to assume the role of spy for the administration, in order to "get something" on student and faculty dissenters. Obviously, in this role his rapport with students is seriously impaired.

The Counselor as Consultant

In view of the many problems discussed, it seems unrealistic to expect the college counselor alone to assist black students. He needs the help and cooperation of numerous others on the campus. Because of the complexity of the black and white problem, it is suggested that the counselor, in addition to his usual role, perform in a consultative capacity. Although he should continue to provide individual and group counseling, lead confrontation and encounter sessions, and meet with parents, he should also consult with campus psychologists, psychiatrists, physicians, and ministers in order to help them delineate their roles in assisting black students to adjust to the college environment, be it predominately white or black. In fact, it is advised that he function as the leader of the college therapeutic team, whenever administratively feasible.

He may also advise other officials who perform significant roles which impinge directly on the black student's perception of the campus environment. He may be a member of the committee which selects campus resource people. Speakers representing all religious, political, and racial views should be permitted to speak to large audiences, both black and white, and to dialogue with small groups of students, integrated and segregated, if such an arrangement is desired by black students for legitimate reasons.

The counselor can also help college officials to reassess their orientation programs, which very often constitute the black student's first impression of the campus. Assisting the administration in the creation of brotherhood microcosms is undoubtedly one of the most vital functions therapeutic professionals can perform on college campuses. This suggests that the counselor is consultant to the academic dean, the housing director, the food service manager, and other officials who are responsible for planning for the freshman's first week on campus.

5

Counseling Negro Adults

Today, counselors relate to Negro adults in a variety of settings. In schools, they come in contact with parents who are concerned about their children's progress; in penal institutions, they help professionals engage in rehabilitative efforts; in the military, they relate to GI's preparing to re-enter civilian life; and in government service, counselors in numerous agencies are servicing black workers with a multitude of problems. In all of these settings, professionals look for guidance and direction on how to work more effectively with Negro counselees. In many ways, relating to Negro adults may be more difficult than counseling adolescents, for the adult has established an identity and a set of values and attitudes more permanent than maturing individuals.

Establishing Rapport

Rapport may be defined as a comfortable and unconstrained relationship of mutual confidence between two or more individuals (Buchheimer & Balogh, 1961). Although some counselors frequently misconstrue it to mean putting the counselee at ease by making small talk (Patterson, 1966), such an approach to this vital aspect of the relationship is not only superficial, but it may also be dangerous, especially if the counselor does not know what "small talk" is appropriate. White counselors who are not familiar with Negroes are often awkward in their attempts to be casual and warm at first meeting. A counselor in a government agency is reported to have inquired of a black counselee about his family: "Say, John, you people don't happen to come from Mississippi, do you?" To this, the counselee replied in the negative. The counselor continued, "You know, you look so much like a boy who used to work for my mother when we lived down in Pascagoula." Needless to say, the counselee was ready to leave the interview before he sat down. The word "boy" and the phrase "you people" are especially offensive to Negroes.

When the counselee makes the contact, the counselor should neither initiate nor encourage small talk which is not germane to the purpose of the relationship. Rapport ensues from the counselor's displaying a real interest in the individual and a willingness to hear him out. Any attempt to immediately establish himself as a "good guy" can set the wrong tone for a beneficial relationship.

Rapport is also a dynamic phenomenon. Even if the counselor is successful, through some sort of artificial behavior, in establishing an emotional bridge at the beginning of the initial interview, there is no assurance that such a bond will remain intact either in the first interview or in those to come. A counseling interview is a continuous exchange of verbal and non-verbal language. Both participants continue to reveal more of themselves to each other. The counselee evaluates the counselor as a person. He comes to understand and sense his values and attitudes through what he says and how he says it. Progressive self-disclosure on the part of either or both participants may enhance or detract from the initially established rapport. As the counselee gets to know the counselor, previous reserve may give way to total acceptance or early mutual respect, and fluidity of expression may grow static.

Whether rapport can be established and maintained frequently depends on the nature of the content to be discussed. In general, personal problems require more trust and confidence than those which pertain to issues which are not threatening to the ego. In the course of a single interview, the counselee can shift from easy acceptance to tacit reserve, depending on the counselor's leads. Although a black counselee might be perfectly willing to talk with a white counselor about problems related to furthering his education, he may resist exploring with the same counselor problems connected with a white supervisor who he thinks is discriminating against him because of his race.

The sex of the counselor and counselee can also effect the nature of the rapport established and maintained. The counseling dyad may consist of several combinations: white male counselor-black male counselee; white female counselor-black male counselee; black male counselor-black male counselee; black female counselor-black male counselee; and so on. In general, white male counselors experience little difficulty relating to black females. In the American society, white men and black women have related well with each other down through history, probably because Negro women have worked for them as domestics and nurse maids.

Negro counselors experience little difficulty establishing rapport with other Negroes. In some cases, however, the relationship bond may become strained because of differences in values, perceptions of the racial problem, and place of birth. If the black counselor indicates to the Negro counselee that he thinks that he is white or fails to demonstrate sufficient understanding of the black problem, rapport may indeed be strained. Also, southern middle-class Negroes, in particular, are often on the defensive with Negroes from other parts of the country, especially if they perceive the outsider to be "putting them down" because of the part of the country in which they live.

There is some reason to believe that the black female counselor can establish a more positive and lasting rapport with the black male than a male counselor can. Coming from homes in which their mothers were the strongest or only parent present, developing males have learned to confide in and trust the female parent. The relationship with their fathers, even those who remain a part of the household, is generally cold, distant, and formal. In general, lower-class Negro male children find it difficult to identify with or to relate to indifferent fathers. Sidney Jourard's (1964) extensive research on self-disclosure indicates that Negro males consistently disclose most to their mothers, and comparatively little, if at all, to their fathers.

The white female counselor-black male counselee dyad is probably fraught with more anxiety than any other possible combination, especially if the male is between the ages of 16 and 30, an age-range sometimes tacitly known as the sexually dangerous period, i.e., for Negro males (Vontress, 1969a). The more the counselee represents the stereotype of the big, black, biological male, the more the counselor is apt to feel uncomfortable relating to him, particularly if she is approximately the same age as the counselee. The white female is the product of a society in which white men continue to ask the perennial question, "Would you want your daughter to marry a Negro?" In the American society, the Negro male is a phobogenic object and a stimulus to anxiety (Fanon, 1967). Thus, it is understandable that the white female, although a counselor, reacts as she does toward some black males.

In general, the counselor, male or female, black or white, should find it easier to establish rapport with Negro females than with black men. The black female has enjoyed a greater degree of equality in the

American society than has the male (Vontress, 1969a). As a result, she accepts herself more readily than does the male. Not only this, but Negro females are accepted and loved more by their mothers than are the males. Since they perceive themselves positively, they accept others with little reservation. Thus, the counselor should find it fairly easy to establish a workable relationship with black women.

Although it is difficult to determine when rapport has been established with a counselee, fluidity of self-disclosure is undoubtedly one index. In this connection, Jourard (1961) indicates that the age of an individual affects self-disclosure tendency. Indeed, age has a sobering effect on all human beings. This is especially true of Negroes (Vontress, 1969a). As they mature, they find that there is no effective way to modify the social and economic conditions which suffocate their very existence. They are forced to dam up their terrible feelings within themselves, denying their agonizing presence or allowing the anger to burn itself out. Therefore, the counselor should find it easier to establish a working relationship with middle-aged Negroes than with young, hostile ones. In particular, it is easier for the counselor to explore with his counselee sensitive topics, probably because there is less at stake for the older person (Birren, 1964). Even so, the older person's resignation to the vicissitudes of life makes it difficult for the therapeutic professional to help him realize a fuller life. Poor down-trodden Negroes are quick to assume a *"Qué será, será"* or "God will provide" attitude.

Another variable affecting the counselor's ability to establish a positive rapport with black people is his accent. For example, Negroes living outside the South generally react with suspicion toward white people with southern drawls. They associate the accent with years of segregation and discrimination. Although a southern drawl may not constitute a permanent rapport barrier, it represents an initial impediment to the development of mutual respect and trust.

Counselor Attitudes

To Carl Rogers (1962), the relationship which the counselor forms with the counselee is the most significant aspect of counseling. It is more important than his knowledge of tests and measurement, the adequacy of his record keeping, the theories he holds, the accuracy with which he is able to predict future behavior, or the university from which he received his degree. A relationship characterized by sensitive and accurate empathy on the part of the counselor; by a counselor congruence or genuineness; by a high degree of regard, respect, and appreciation for the counselee by the counselor; and by the absence of conditionality in that regard will have a great probability of being an effective, growth-promoting relationship.

Empathy

Achieving a positive level of attitudinal conditions may be difficult in counseling Negroes, because it is a matter of common experience that individuals do not find it easy to establish empathy with those unlike themselves (Vontress, 1970). Empathy implies that one feels as if he were experiencing someone else's feelings as his own. He sees, feels, responds, and understands as if he were, in fact, the other person.

To a great extent, emphathy is a process of identifying and incorporating one's self with another person. When one identifies, he projects his being into others; when he incorporates, he introjects the other person or persons into himself. Both phases are ways in which the individual comes to sense the reality of the experiences of others. The counselor who brings to the therapeutic encounter his own personal bias against racial and ethnic minorities will not be able to empathize with his inner-city counselees, for his racial hang-ups will intrude directly or indirectly, rendering impotent his professional skills.

To overcome racial hang-ups, or any hang-ups for that matter, is not easy, for counselors, like members of the population at large, are products of their culture. Thus, all too often they unconsciously make their own tastes and demands for excellence and perfection the measure of all goodness, pronouncing all that is broadly different from them imperfect and low or of secondary value (Lee, 1966). Perforce, counselors who work in the inner-city do a lot of soul-searching. They look at themselves a great deal, and in so doing, they may tip in the other direction. That is, there develops the considerable danger of their over identifying with the black counselee and feeling too sympathetic to be of assistance or of retaining residual prejudice about which they feel guilty (Heine, 1950).

Congruence

Rogers points out further that personal growth is facilitated when the counselor is a real person and when in the relationship with the counselee he is genuine and without "front" or facade. To be sure, this is difficult for most people, as Shakespeare suggested when he pointed out that "all the world's a stage, and all the men and women merely players." Undeniably, individuals do wear personas. Even so, a counselor's false face may impede his counseling attempts, for, to a considerable degree, effective counseling depends on the ability of the counselor to permit himself to become a part of the total counseling situation. The counselor must know what he is doing and why. This is hardly possible, unless he understands to some degree his own psychodynamics and cultural conditioning.

In some ways, achieving such an understanding may be more difficult for Negro counselors than for their white counterparts. As members of the black bourgeois, Negro counselors have a problem in authenticating themselves (Broyard, 1950). Estranged from whites, they are also alienated from themselves. Since their companions are a mirror in which they see themselves as ugly, they must reject themselves; they must hate themselves unconsciously, because they are black and thus different.

In attempting to elude their self-hatred, they, in effect, lose themselves in the shuffle. Resting their entire cause and social status on white recognition and acceptance, black Anglo-Saxons find themselves doomed forever to wear a mask, so to speak, especially when in the presence of whites (Hare, 1965). In their upward movement, they lead uncomfortable lives. Cut off from the white world and avoiding Negroes lower than themselves, they live and behave the way they think whites want them to. In so doing, they often outdo those whom they imitate. Thus, it is not uncommon to encounter black professionals who are less accepting of lower-class blacks than are their white counterparts. In this connection, Brown (1950) reports that Negro social workers are likely to be more punitive toward counselees of their own race than toward white counselees. Deviation from accepted standards in a member of their own race is often seen as a reflection on the race as a whole and, more importantly, themselves.

Positive Regard

Rogers goes on to point out that growth and changes are more likely to occur if the counselor is experiencing a warm, positive, acceptant attitude toward the counselee as he is, not as he will be or could be. This means that the counselor accepts the ugly, black, foul-talking individual; that he accepts the angry, embittered counselee. As social and economic conditions continue to deteriorate in ghettos in this country, inhabitants of these areas are forced to adjust to their terrible situations. As they shift their values and attitudes toward themselves, toward others unlike themselves, and toward society as a whole, the counselor may find it progressively difficult to accept lower-class Negro counselees, especially those who live in the inner city.

For example, the cries of Black Power are extremely disconcerting to most middle-class observers. White "friends" flee in horror and frustration from civil rights organizations, and race relations are at a low ebb in this country. The intimacy and goodwill which existed between the races when the Negro demonstrated willingness to "stay in his place" show signs of evaporation now that black people indicate that they are no longer willing to accept their place (Killian & Grigg, 1964). In fact, there is no indication that more than a minority of white people, either in the South or the North, are yet prepared psychologically to extend either friendship or equality to the Negro.

Even if race were not a factor in the consideration of positive regard, class differences might intrude in any attempt to relate to Negroes. To achieve a high degree of positive regard for people who are different, the counselor must learn more about their way of life, their ethnic and social values and attitudes, and he will have to overcome his own prejudices.

Unconditionality of Positive Regard

Positive regard, *per se,* is not enough. The counselor does not enjoy the luxury of choosing his counselees or those whom he wishes to accept completely. Middleton (1963) points out that alienation is pervasive among Negroes in this country — and there is reason to believe that he is right. Many ghetto inhabitants perceive their lives to be empty and hopeless and their activities normless; for many of them, trying to make a living is futile. Thus, they are forced to be adept at "hustling," at "making it" in any way they can.

In great urban areas, counselors find themselves relating to dope addicts, criminals, mothers given to serial mating, and pushers. Those who call themselves counselors are put to the test in accepting such individuals. In fact, the counselor may find his own values being challenged. He may be referred to as "sick," "a square," and the like. Should he write off such people as hopeless, and send them from his office or place of work? Of late, some white counselors indicate that they are harassed not only by their counselees, but by their black co-workers as well. Often, their colleagues tell them that they "don't understand" or "can't understand," simply because they are white. Unfortunately, some white counselors are beginning to believe it. Little do they or their Negro co-workers realize that if black counselees perceive white counselors as the enemy, they are apt to see Negro professionals as something far worse — collaborators with the enemy. The problems of relating to lower-class Negro counselees are somewhat the same for Negro counselors as they are for their white counterparts.

Assuming that the counselor exemplifies and honestly views his counselees with all the attitudinal ingredients discussed, there is still the problem of the counselee's perception of the counselor. It is not enough for him to declare himself to be warm, accepting, and sensitive to all people. What he is must be communicated to the counselee. How this is done is not clear. However, one thing seems definite. An inner-city person can size up a counselor in a very few minutes. It does little good for the counselor to verbally declare himself a "good guy." If he is one, the counselee will know it. Verbalizing what he is, is a terrible and damaging waste of words.

The Counseling Interview

Although it is not the purpose here to review various techniques which counselors generally use in achieving the goals of counseling, it seems appropriate to indicate some potentially sensitive areas in the relationship with black people of which the counselor should be aware.

Getting Off to a Good Start

In general, counselors agree that counseling should take place in complete privacy. Even so, exceptions to the rule should be possible. If the counselor or counselee feels uncomfortable for whatever reason, when they are completely enclosed, provisions for semi-privacy should be available. For example, it has been noted that some white female counselors may feel uneasy in conference with young black men (Vontress, 1969b). In such a case, she should be able to leave her office door open or ajar, for her anxiety is apt to be detected by the counselee and therefore detract from the relationship. If the counselor thinks that the counselee might feel uncomfortable with the door closed, he or she should simply ask, "Would you like for me to close the door?" not "May I close the door?" The latter question is apt to get a positive response, not because the counselee wishes to respond as such, but because it would be impolite to say "No!"

How the counselor greets the counselee at first meeting is also crucial. Some therapeutic professionals, realizing the need to eliminate social distance as soon as possible and to establish a positive relationship bridge, may address the counselee by his first name. For a white counselee to call a black person by his first name in the initial interview may be perceived by the minority person as disrespect. In the past, whites in many parts of the country seldom extended blacks the courtesy of addressing them by "Mr.," "Mrs.," or "Miss." For this reason, the counselor should put a handle on the individual's name, until he is given permission to do otherwise. After an initial rapport has been established, he may then ask the individual if he may address him by his first name.

Seating arrangement is also important to consider. The counselor and the counselee should be seated so that the client does not have to look the counselor "dead in the eye," unless he so chooses. Such an arrangement is probably more important in counseling Negroes than it is with whites, because in the past, blacks in the South tacitly understood that it was taboo to look directly at whites. This was especially true in the case of black men talking with white women. Also, not looking another person directly in the eye is a sign of courtesy and deference in some quarters of the country.

Some blacks may freeze if the counselor, especially if he happens to be white, makes bodily contact with them. While most blacks, middle-class or lower-class, young adults or older ones, will accept without hesitation a handshake, many will find offensive a slap on the back or a pat on the shoulder. This can probably be explained by the frequent habit of some Southern whites in the past to put their hands on or to rub the heads of blacks, especially black men. This was and is perceived as condescending behavior.

In relating to Negro counselees, white counselors should be polite and accepting, but not overly friendly in the first interview. Undue affability on the part of a representative of a people who have not always exemplified such behavior is apt to be perceived as phony. Although the counselor should make no attempt to pretend that the Negro counselee is not Negro, he should be careful to use a racial designation, when necessary, which is not offensive to the individual. Today, persons of African descent generally use three terms to refer to themselves: Negro, black, and colored. If the counselor uses one which is not preferred by the counselee, he runs the risk of offending him. In order to avoid this possibility, the counselor should either wait to hear which designation the counselee uses or ask him directly for his preference.

Structuring the Relationship

According to Shertzer and Stone (1968), structuring refers to the way the counselor "defines the nature, limits, roles, and goals within the counseling relationship." Harrison and Carek (1966) point out that it is especially important to communicate to the counselee what the relationship entails and how it differs from other relationships which he has had with other authority figures. Structuring is especially important in counseling Negroes, for the expectations and preferences of counselees in counseling and psychotherapy are learned and are therefore culturally determined and conditioned, as Patterson (1958) has indicated. Middle-class people have from infancy a continuing series of relationships with professionals and friends who assist them in some way: the doctor, lawyer, and certainly parents and siblings. These contacts are, in the main, verbalizing relationships. The roles of the assister and the assisted are clearly understood. With lower-class individuals, such roles are not as clear-cut. Therefore, structuring the counseling relationship is particularly important in counseling them (Vontress, 1969b).

In general, therapeutic professionals are most familiar with middle-class Americans. Although the counseling dyad approximates other types of relationships which people have with other helping professionals, it differs significantly in terms of the responsibilities and roles of those involved. Black people have been accustomed to going to doctors, who "do something" to them to make them well again; to teachers, who give them advice; to their bosses, who tell them what to do; and to many other authority figures who talk to, rather than with them. Therefore, it is natural that the uninitiated would expect the same from counselors.

Although some structuring should be done at the very beginning of the relationship, it is not suggested that the counselor belabor the point. He should structure as he goes along. If, for example, a black employee comes to an Equal Employment Opportunity counselor in a governmental agency, complaining that he is being discriminated against and demanding that the counselor get him a promotion immediately, the counselor can at this point indicate that it is not within his power to provide him with a promotion, but to help him decide the proper course of action, in view of his complaint. In other words, the EEO counselor delays most of the structuring until the counselee makes illegitimate demands on him.

Structuring the counseling relationship with middle-class Negroes may proceed the same as it would with middle-class whites. However, with lower-class blacks, the counselor should be more sensitive to this aspect of the relationship. In general, people from the ghetto are suspicious of a lot of talk. In interpersonal relationships, they often perceive people who talk too much for no apparent reason as individuals who are trying to "pull the wool over your eyes" or as persons who have an illicit interest in them.

Hostility

Because of the present state of black and white rapport in this country, white counselors may feel strong hostility being directed toward them by their black counselees. This may be attributed to the fact that even though segregation and discrimination are no longer the problems they used to be, many black people are insistent on redressing historical wrongs inflicted upon their forebears. For some, their hostility is simply an expression of their attempt to cover up feelings of inadequacy, defeat, and hopelessness that come from having been denied equal opportunity for so long.

Although not all blacks are imbued with hostility, the counselor should be aware of its possible presence, either overt or passive. Northern ghetto inhabitants are apt to express their feelings more openly than Southern Negroes, who have learned to suppress their true sentiments toward people whom they perceive to be their oppressors. This suggests that a counselee who is quiet and appears to be uncommunicative may, in fact, be expressing hostility.

If the counselor suspects that the counselee's hostility is impeding the counseling process, he may explore this possibility with him. Sometimes hostility can be minimized by talking about it. However, how these feelings are brought up and discussed is critical. Obviously, there is no one way to deal with the situation. Some counselors may wish to ignore what they perceive to be hostility and proceed to help the individual with his immediate concern, realizing that "action" may go further in eliminating such feelings than a great deal of talk, which, after all, is inimical to the ghetto life style.

Resistance

Closely related to hostility is resistance, which, as simply defined by Greenson (1967), means opposition to the goals and procedures of counseling. Although the sources of resistance are many, as Brammer and Shostrom (1968) point out, it is suspected that in the case of the Negro male, the phenomenon is directly related to his reluctance to allow the counselor to penetrate his innermost ego defenses. In general, lower-class males learn an exaggerated aggressiveness, an iron-clad facade to protect a feeble ego, erected in part through an effort to counter the threatening effects of the black matriarchy (Devine, 1964). Therefore, they invest an inordinate amount of physical and psychological energy in asserting a unidimensional image of maleness. Basic to their facade is "cooling it," or "keeping it to yourself."

Thus, this manly attitude is in opposition to counseling, which requires that the counselee reveal himself to another. The black male is most reluctant to expose his real self to anyone, even to his closest friends or spouse. To allow the facade to be stripped away, even for a moment, is to be left defenseless against a hostile world, in which people will "do you in." Therefore, it is important to "keep up your dukes."

During maturing years, the black male develops around him an iron-clad facade designed to conceal his insecurity and frustration resulting from not being able to play the social male role so highly prized in the American society (Vontress, 1969a). Even though the wall is difficult to penetrate, the counselor can eventually pierce it; but he must be gentle in the process, for to destroy this masculine facade without replacing it with something equally durable is to destroy a human being whose ancestors have been trod upon for more than three generations. Black male resistance in the counseling interview usually means that much more time is required to assist him in any way, especially with personal problems, than it is with a black female.

It is important to point out, however, that the "playing it cool" syndrome is primarily characteristic of lower-class black men. In general, middle-class Negroes lower their defenses much more readily. Many become lachrymose without apparent reason, as Grier and Cobbs (1968) indicate. They are so overwhelmed by their predicament in a country where, in spite of their socio-economic status, they are virtually powerless to control their destiny, that they actually cry for themselves. Thus, the counselor should encounter few resistances in their relationship with them and, of course, with black females in general, who, as was indicated earlier, enjoy a life with relatively few restrictions, at least as compared to their male counterparts.

Reflection

According to Brammer and Shostrom (1968), reflection refers to the counselor's attempt to restate in fresh language the words, feelings, and attitudes verbalized by the counselee. Attempting to reflect properly in a counseling relationship with black counselees may present several problems for the white counselor. In order to reflect skillfully, the counselor must be completely familiar with the language and gestures of his counselees. It also requires that he be able to identify with their experiences and feelings.

White counselors and, to a certain extent, some black ones are so far removed from the realities of the lives of lower-class blacks that they cannot understand the nuances of their language, to say nothing of their experiences in the ghetto. The ghetto in this country constitutes a sub-culture with unique values and attitudes. An outsider finds it difficult to communicate with clarity with its inhabitants. Although many middle-class blacks declare that they came from the same area, they now speak with a different accent, because subtleties of the language have changed since they lived there.

To reflect properly means that the counselor must be able to understand not only verbalized language, but body language as well. Take, for example, the black counselee who said to the white counselor that he was going "to go upside" the head of his supervisor. The counselor, never having heard the expression before, said, "I'm afraid I don't understand. You mean that you are going to talk with your boss?" "No man, I'm gonna knock the hell out of him if he don't get off my back." Needless to say, "get off my back" may have also been foreign to the counselor.

In order to reflect properly the content and feelings of the black person, the counselor must have a firsthand understanding of his life as he now experiences it, not as the counselor imagines or remembers it to be. Mistakes in reflections of ideas, feelings, and experiences often constitute the final breaking point of the little rapport existing between the counselor and the counselee.

It is not suggested that the counselor try to use the same vernacular as the counselee. Many middle-class counselors often ask the question, "Should I talk in the language of the ghetto?" A proper response to such a question is, "When in Rome, speak Italian, if you know Italian; if not, speak whatever language you know." In general a counselor who attempts to use a vernacular with which he is not comfortable will come across to the native speaker, at least the one from the black ghetto, as a phony at best and a fool at worst.

Transference

Greenson (1967) describes transference as a therapeutic phenomenon in which the "helped" reacts to the "helper" as though he were a person in his past. Whether conscious or unconscious, it is nevertheless a form of resistance in the counseling relationship (Harrison & Carek, 1966). In the black and white counseling dyad, transference may be a real problem, for the black counselee brings to the relationship all of the perceptions which he has or has had of whites. Almost all Negroes in this country have had unpleasant experiences with whites in one setting or another. In fact, it is nearly impossible for a black person to go through a single day of his life without somehow being reminded that he is different, that he is inferior, that he is black.

Although in the white-white counseling dyad, transference may be either positive or negative, it is fair to say that in the white-black dyad, it is almost always apt to be negative. In addition to the transference feelings stemming from the counselee's family figures, there are also intense emotions derived from his feelings toward whites in general (Greenson, 1967). On first meeting the counselor, the black counselee sees the counselor as a white person, period. Thus, he reacts to him initially as he reacts or has reacted to all white persons in his past: with reserve, suspicion, fear, or doubt. This is especially so in the case of black males, who have experienced the most severe disenfranchisement in the American society.

Countertransference

Countertransference is often defined as the counselor's reaction to the counselee, because of previous relationships in his, the counselor's past. As Greenson (1967) indicates, countertransference reactions can lead to persistent inappropriate behavior toward the counselee in the form of constant misunderstandings. Black-white transference and countertransference difficulties are compounded by the differences in the backgrounds of the therapeutic participants.

Although there are many signs of transference in white-white counseling dyads, two of them which may exist in the white-black relationship need to be singled out here. One of these is the "great white father syndrome." The white counselor is overly anxious to prove to or to reassure the black counselee that he is all powerful or that he is not like all "those other whites." Another indication of countertransference may be the counselor's overzealous concern for the counselee's welfare (Harrison & Carek, 1966). Often, his wish to assist beyond the call of duty is an attempt to atone for the sins of his race or for his own guilt feelings about personal residuals of prejudice towards blacks.

Because of the nature of the culture in which the counselor developed, it is virtually impossible for him to be devoid of some of the traditional feelings toward blacks. Therefore, his very attempt to be objective, detached, warm, and empathetic may be an indication that he is trying too hard to be what he really is not and that he is protesting too much.

The intent here is not to provide prescriptions, but to call to the counselor's attention, especially the dominant group professional, some of the nuances of the black-white therapeutic relationship. To do so is not to deny that countertransference problems may not exist in the black-black dyad as well. However, the likelihood is much more remote because of sameness of race. This fact seems crucial, since initial transference and countertransference impediments are generally more difficult to resolve than those which may develop at later stages of the therapeutic encounter.

Summary

Throughout the monograph, counseling has been defined as an interpersonal relationship. Therefore, in this chapter, an attempt has been made to highlight some of the relationship problems which can develop in the counseling dyad with black adult counselees. Although the chapter is entitled "Counseling Negro Adults," it should be clear that some of the same relationship problems may exist in counseling adolescents and college students. Therefore, the psychological aspect of the counseling interview discussed should not be construed as being only problematic in relating to adults.

6

The Use of Tests with Negroes

During the last few years, perhaps no issue has been more discussed in the educational, psychological, and sociological literature than the use of standardized tests with the so-called disadvantaged, a frequent euphemism for black people. Although the discussion continues and even though authorities generally agree that Negroes usually do not do as well on standardized psychological tests as do members of the modal population, tests are still used in schools, employment services, and business and industry to screen people into and out of various categories. They are used to determine who is assigned to certain curricula, who goes to college, who gets scholarships, who is hired for certain kinds of jobs, and frequently, to determine who constitutes a security risk.

Authorities enumerate a variety of reasons why the disadvantaged do poorly on tests. Most of the explanations can be subsumed under one heading, *cultural differences*. Whenever people are separated from one another for whatever reason, they develop unique ways of establishing and maintaining rapport with their environment. Even though Negroes consider themselves Americans, they at the same time identify strongly with "The Race." A black child grows up not just in the American culture, but more importantly, he matures in a Negro subculture. This subculture, like the American umbrella culture, consists of all the folkways, habit patterns, and various *modus operandi* which members of a human society develop in order to cope with the environment and to interact with their fellows (Crites, 1969).

The demands and expectations of the subculture are generally more determinant of an individual's behavior than are those of the umbrella culture. It is the culture in which the infant is first socialized. The child's initial development of a superego is a direct result of his immediate subculture, not the culture at large. He first internalizes the restraints imposed upon him by his parents, who represent, in the case of the Negro, the black subculture; when he ventures from home, he inculcates the values and attitudes of his neighborhood peers, who are also usually black. Attitudes, values, and motivational patterns acquired during impressionable years become powerful forces which continue to direct much of his behavior throughout his lifetime.

Today, blacks and whites are more separated from each other physically and psychologically than ever before in the history of this country. The exodus of whites to urban peripheries and the static density of blacks in inner-cities has, indeed, created two separated and unequal societies, members of which think and react differently. Each society develops distinct values, attitudes, motivational patterns, and other aspects of human behavior generally transmitted by a culture. Even though the cultural differences are quite apparent, schools, whether located in the ghetto or suburbia, remain or attempt to remain transmitters of the modal culture in terms of their demands and expectations of students, and in terms of the tools used to categorize individuals who pass through their portals.

The color of the Negro's skin defines an aspect of his subculture, not so much because of manifest physical differences which set him apart from the dominant population, but because of social reactions of the majority group toward the color (Crites, 1969). To say this is not to suggest that all black people are separate and therefore unequal. The extent to which blacks are assimilated appears to be the extent to which they can compete favorably with whites. Assimilation is generally considered in terms of fusion of members of the minority group into the national or dominant culture. However, the degree of fusion is important. If the fusion implies absorption of values and attitudes and free access to community participation and total inculcation of the dimensions of culture, then assimilation may be thought of as being complete. In this connection, it is important to make a distinction between assimilation and identification. For some time now, middle-class blacks have identified with middle-class whites, without being assimilated. They remain, for the most part, outsiders attempting to approximate the behavior of people whom they do not completely understand or accept. Even so, middle-class Negroes compete more favorably with the modal white population than do lower-class blacks, most of whom have considerably less exposure to the values, goals, and attitudes of the white group with whom competition is necessary.

Implications for Testing Negroes

In the case of black people, cultural isolation has had telling effects on their test taking behavior and subsequently on test results. By dominant group middle-class standards, Negroes are less verbal, generally because of the crippling effects of deprived homes and poor schools; more unaccustomed to and often fearful of strangers, especially white ones who, for example, administer tests to them; debilitated by a poor self-concept; less competitive in intellectual pursuits; less conforming to middle-class norms; and generally resistant to authority figures (SPSSI, 1964). In a nutshell, black people do not do well on tests for the same reason that they do poorly in school. They either cannot read well enough to understand the items, or the whole business of taking tests is not relevant to their lives as they perceive them.

Proficiency Tests

In psychometric literature, tests have been assigned a variety of names. Under the broad category of proficiency tests may be lumped instruments sometimes referred to as aptitude, achievement, developmental, and so forth. As Cronback (1960) suggests, it is probably more important to consider how the tests are used than it is to be concerned with what they are called. Clear distinctions among achievement, scholastic ability, and aptitude tests are not easy to make, since such tests often cover essentially similar content (Shertzer & Peters, 1965). For example, if a test is used to determine where a student is *now*, it is generally called an achievement test; if it is used to predict future behavior, it is referred to as an aptitude test.

In general, all such tests, no matter what they are called, require reading. In testing black students in a preponderance of the nation's ghetto schools, proficiency tests should be referred to simply as reading tests, for if a student cannot read the test items, how can the results be indicative of anything but reading ability. For example, it is hardly useful to administer a social studies proficiency test with a readability level of 8.3 to a student who reads at the fourth grade level and then conclude that a low score represents insufficient performance or knowledge in social studies.

Intelligence Tests

It seems reasonable to say that there is hardly consensus among psychologists as to what intelligence is. Since there is a variety of standardized tests labelled "intelligence tests," it appears that intelligence is what an intelligence test measures. Thus, a consideration of what they measure is appropriate.

According to Mehrens (1969), most educational institutions use group tests to measure intelligence. These, like proficiency tests, require that the examinee be able to read at the level at which the test is written if he is to obtain a score higher than one would by randomly responding to items. Even if the examinee can read adequately enough to interpret the language in which the items are written, cultural differences may affect the results. In a society where subcultural groups are exposed to disparate experiences, which most paper-and-pencil intelligence tests attempt to sample or tap, black youngsters, as members of a distinct racial group, are severely handicapped. The tests demand verbal fluency, speed, motivation, and appropriate values and attitudes, all of which are related to the demands and expectations of the individual's subculture. It should be understandable that many black youngsters and adults show up poorly on paper-and-pencil intelligence tests.

It is also important to consider the effect of the examiner on the results of intelligence tests when black students are tested in groups or individually. Black people, especially lower-class ones, have had limited experience associating with whites in relationships other than those in which whites were perceived as the superior and blacks the inferior. A white person administering a group test to black people can adversely affect test results.

This is perhaps even more influential in a testing dyad than in a group setting. The black person brings to the relationship anxieties and unconscious attitudes and feelings about whites in general. The white professional, as a product of his culture, also brings to the relationship attitudes and perceptions, conscious and unconscious, of black people. These, too, intrude in the testing dyad. Individual testing requires an amicable rapport the same as does counseling. Unless a positive relationship bridge is established and maintained during the individual testing session, one is justified in raising questions about the results obtained.

Personality Tests

Lazarus (1963) defines personality as "the dynamic organization within the individual of those psychological systems that determine his unique adjustments to his environment." If one accepts this definition and at the same time acknowledges that Negroes constitute a subcultural group in the American society, it would seem tenable to reject all personality tests normed and standardized on the modal population. Negroes, as a distinct disenfranchised group, have perforce endured severe adjustment problems in the American environment. In adjusting to their immediate subculture, they have used mechanisms which may be considered unique. Thus, the norms used in constructing personality assessment instruments for the dominant population may be questioned when applied to nonwhites.

In recent years, several writers have discussed the unique aspects of the Negro personality (Brazziel, 1964; Karon, 1958; Grier & Cobbs, 1968; and Vontress, 1966). They have all indicated the unique adjustment problems which blacks have to make, or try to make, in a society which denies them what is generally taken for granted by whites. Further, they have indicated that black youngsters must adjust to their immediate environments, usually before considering the demands and expectations of the larger society. If there is a Negro personality, and there is good reason to believe that there is, then instruments normed and standardized on the modal white population are useless for assessing the personality of black people.

Even if a black person in the American society could completely elude the effects of the inferior status assigned him, there is still some question as to whether he can escape his cultural heritage which is rooted in slavery, a cultural heritage which he cannot escape, for every other black person somehow reminds him of his past, of what he could have been or of what his forebears were.

If it could be assumed that cultural differences do not affect personality, reading ability, especially on paper-and-pencil personality instruments, is still apt to affect the meaningfulness of any results obtained. Not only this, but the influence of the psychologist or the examiner must be considered, if he happens to be white. The clinician who attempts to assess the Negro personality impressionistically needs to be aware not only of the unique behavior of the subculture, but he must have an understanding of his own cultural conditioning toward black people as well. Attempts to assess the black personality in the manner of or with the same standards or criteria used with the modal white population is almost certain to lead to false diagnoses.

Interest Inventories

An interest may be defined as a feeling of intentness, concern, or curiosity about something. The acquisition of interests is one aspect of the process of socialization. As such, they are significantly influenced by the total environment in which the child develops, by his opportunities for try-outs (Super & Crites, 1962), by the figures with whom he identifies, and by a wide range of experiences which trigger phantasizing about adulthood.

The acquisition of vocational interests is facilitated by travel, by hobbies, by exposure to people who work at a variety of jobs, and by the school one attends. A school with well-equipped science laboratories, displays, and a good library contributes to the development of a wider array of interests than one in which such educational assets are lacking or inadequate. Simply put, when a child has not had an opportunity to gain satisfaction or rewards from certain pursuits, he is not likely to show interest in these areas (SPSSI, 1964).

Therefore, the use of interest inventories to determine the interests of Negroes may be questioned for at least two reasons. First, Negroes, having been isolated for so long from the mainstream of the modal society, have been denied the opportunity to develop well-defined interests. Secondly, it seems justifiable to question the use of both the Kuder and Strong inventories, because of their readability. Super & Crites (1962) report that the grade reading level of the Kuder is 8.4 and that of the Strong is 10.4. That a majority of black high school and college students have depressed reading scores is well known; therefore, the likelihood of their scores being questionable on the Kuder and Strong for this reason is great.

Recommendations

A case can be made for the discontinuation of the use of standardized tests for assessing non-assimilated racial and ethnic minorities in the United States. Although there are no clear indices of assimilation, language facility is undoubtedly one indication. Here, language is used in its broadest sense to suggest its role in the transmission of culture from one generation to another. Language, as a major aspect of a culture, serves as its barometer to reflect changes in cultural demands and expectations, however subtle (Cohen, 1956). Thus, those who observe that Negroes are verbally destitute, and somehow connect the destitution with depressed scores on standardized tests, overly simplify a complex problem. It would be more accurate to recognize that language differences as reflected between blacks and whites in this country are another indication of a more global difference, cultural. Variations in the subtleties of language are but one example of the gross differences.

In spite of their recognized inappropriateness for segments of non-assimilated groups in the United States, standardized tests are apt to remain a major screening tool, until a suitable replacement is found. Therefore, a few guidelines are in order for testing Negroes.

1. The counselor should determine informally the degree to which the individual is assimilated in the American culture, before administering a standardized test to him. This may be done through counseling, either in a dyad or group.

2. Rapport must be established with the examinee, whether he is being tested individually or in a group. Whenever possible, the examiner should be of the same race as the examinee.

3. Examiners with regional accents which put Negroes on guard should not be used. White people with Southern accents are apt to produce anxiety and/or hostility in black examinees, both of which may affect test results.

4. The examiner should determine formally or informally the reading level of the examinee before administering a standardized test to him. If the reading level of the test is beyond that of the individual's reading ability, there is little use in proceeding with the testing.

5. Since motivation affects test behavior and results, it is recommended that Negroes be prepared for test sessions. Individual and group counseling may encourage potential examinees to want to do well on the tests.

6. In order to insure optimum testing conditions, it is recommended that the size of the testing group be kept small. The examiner might try testing in groups of ten. Herding groups of fifty, one hundred, or two hundred students into a large testing arena is most undesirable.

7. Many test batteries require from six to eight hours to administer. Individuals who lack motivation and interest in test taking find it difficult to endure such long sessions. Therefore, it is recommended that the duration of testing be segmented whenever possible. Instead of giving a six hour test in a single day, perhaps it might be segmented into a single hour for six days.

Obviously, these are but a few recommendations that could be made for testing Negro adolescents and adults. Ideally, an impressionistic approach to assessing blacks should be used. However, such an approach requires a well-trained psychologist who is familiar with the Negro subculture. Such an approach is also too time-consuming to be feasible in most settings.

7

Summary

Throughout this monograph, counseling has been defined as an interpersonal relationship between two or more individuals, one of whom is perceived to be able to assist the other(s) in some way. Crucial to the relationship is the manner in which the *helped* perceives the *helper*. Rapport is vital, if the encounter is to be beneficial to the counselee. An attempt has been made to indicate that in counseling Negroes in the American society, strained rapport is the basic impediment to the realization of counseling goals.

Although impaired rapport has been cited as the basic problem, it has not been suggested that all Negroes react the same in a counseling relationship. In general, it is easier to establish a beneficial relationship with black females than with black males. Socio-economic differences have also been noted. Negro middle-class people relate more positively with white counselors than their lower-class counterparts. The nature of the rapport is also influenced by the age of the counselee. Generally, adolescents and young adults express hostility more readily either by reserve or openly, than do older Negroes.

Differences encountered in establishing rapport with individuals in various regions of the country have also been mentioned. The white counselor should find it easier to establish a workable relationship with Southern-born Negroes than with those born and reared in the

North, probably because individuals outside the South express hostility which is based in part on disillusionment and unfulfilled expectations. Also, the black person still living in the South has learned throughout the years to conceal his pent-up hatred of whites and the system which overtly denies him equality.

The race and sex of the counselor and counselee have also been discussed. The establishment and maintenance of rapport with black females are easier than with black males, since the latter may erect defense mechanisms to protect a feeble ego, a product of their severe disenfranchisement in the American society. It has been suggested that the counseling dyad of a white female and a young black male may be especially anxiety-producing, particularly for the counselor, because of her cultural conditioning.

In general, strained rapport in the counseling relationship and the inappropriateness of techniques employed by the counselor are resultant of black and white cultural differences. The extent to which the black counselee is assimilated is the extent to which the white counselor should encounter problems resulting from racial differences. Although there has been little discussion of the dynamics of the black-black counseling dyad, it appears that the degree to which the black counselor is perceived by the black counselee to identify with whites is the extent to which he may also experience relationship difficulties. The Negro counselee generally approaches the black counselor expecting greater understanding and acceptance, just because of the counselor's race. If his expectations are not borne out, he may assault the counselor with epithets suggesting that he is "whitewashed."

Cultural difference has been cited continuously as the reason why black adolescents encounter academic problems in school, why they need special assistance in preparing for and applying for college admission, and a major reason why they have difficulty succeeding in college. In the chapter on counseling Negro adults, some typical counseling techniques were discussed to illustrate the counselor's need to modify counseling procedures, if he is to be successful in counseling blacks. Briefly, an attempt was made to indicate how cultural variations also invalidate the effective use of most standardized tests with Negroes.

Implications for Counselor Training

Implied in the foregoing chapters is the need for an innovative approach to pre-service and in-service training of counselors. Basic to the reason for concern about counseling blacks are cultural differences between whites and blacks in this country. Therefore, a new kind of training is urgently needed for white counselors. In general, the content of counselor training should include the history of blacks in the United States, the sociology of blacks, and the psychological results of being black in a society perceived by a majority of Negro Americans as being anti-black.

Sensitivity type training is also needed. However, the current approach to such group encounters is not recommended. These have usually consisted of groups of blacks and whites coming together for the purpose of telling and learning it "like it is." After such sessions, both racial groups frequently go away more frustrated than before, because the blacks sense that the whites do not, cannot, or do not want to understand their problems. Whites often depart with a sense of increased frustration and reinforced prejudice. In general, blacks are tired of group experiences in which they perceive their role to be that of educating whites to "the way it really is."

Instead of sensitivity type group experiences for whites, it is suggested that they live in the ghetto for several days or weeks to get a feel of what it is like to be black, to understand the real Negro, not the black person perceived on television, in the movies, or on the job. Negroes necessarily wear false faces for a variety of reasons. Sometimes, it is to delude themselves from their own misery; often, it is to deceive whites. If white counselors want to acquire the ability to assist Negro counselees from an internal frame of reference, living on location is a prerequisite.

Counselor educators need to restudy their counselor education curricula and procedures for training counselors. In general, programs throughout the country can be characterized more as guidance rather than counseling programs. Guidance implies, especially when the adjective "group" is placed in front of it, the imparting of information to a group of people. Such an activity requires little knowledge of the clientele. Counseling, a more subtle and sensitive relationship, is a far more difficult activity. That is why more thought must be given to training persons who are presently being graduated from universities with degrees which make them think that they are indeed counselors.

Counselor educators interested in training professionals to relate to black people should not only consider revamping their curricula for relevance, but they should also recruit staff who know Negroes first hand. These may or may not be black people. In fact, they may or may not have college degrees, certainly not Ph.D.'s. If the goal of the training is to help professionals understand the people in question, then "natives" should be brought on board, not people who think they know the natives. This, after all, is the method employed by the Peace Corps.

Actually, there is some doubt that counselor education programs as they are presently constituted can even begin to do the job needed. What is needed is an undergraduate program designed to prepare individuals to counsel minority group people in our society. The present supply of counselors is drawn almost completely from the teaching profession, a cadre of people who are charged with preserving and transmitting the *status quo*. Individuals so inclined are not the most flexible persons to make into counselors for whites or blacks. Also, there is some doubt that the most sensitive and dedicated counselor educators can ever transform such persons into helping professionals with the ability to relate to angry blacks.

An undergraduate counselor training program is needed badly. Intensive specialized courses should begin in the junior year. The curriculum should consist of lectures and seminars in the behavioral sciences, courses dealing with the nature and needs of blacks, and the techniques of relating to individuals in a helping situation. However, the most significant aspect of the program should be the students' experiences *in situ*. They should spend some time living and learning in the black community. Some of their teachers should be individuals who live and work among black people every day. In fact, such individuals should be employed by universities in the business of training counselors, whether they have the usual academic credentials or not. Unless some imagination is infused into counselor education programs in this country, counselors as they are presently known are apt to become obsolete and irrelevant, especially in the eyes of blacks.

BIBLIOGRAPHY

Ausubel, D. P., "Ego Development among Segregated Negro Children." *Mental Hygiene*, Vol. 42, 1958, pp. 362–369.

Ausubel, D. P., and Ausubel, P., "Ego Development among Segregated Negro Children." In A. H. Passow (Ed.), *Education in Depressed Areas*. New York: Teachers College, 1963.

Bell, R. R., "Lower-class Negro Mothers' Aspirations for their Children." *Social Forces*, Vol. 43, 1963, pp. 493–500.

Berger, E. M., "The Relationship between Expressed Acceptance of Self and Expressed Acceptance of Others." *Journal of Abnormal and Social Psychology*, Vol. 47, 1952, pp. 778–783.

Birren, J. E., *The Psychology of Aging*." Englewood Cliffs, N.J.: Prentice-Hall, 1964.

Brammer, L. M., and Shostrom, E., *Therapeutic Psychology*, 2nd ed. Englewood Cliffs, N.J.: Prentice-Hall, 1968.

Brazziel, W. F., "Correlates of Southern Negro Personality." *Journal of Social Issues*, Vol. 20, 1964, pp. 46–53.

Brody, E. B., "Social Conflict and Schizophrenic Behavior in Young Negro Males." *Psychiatry*, Vol. 24, 1961, pp. 337–346.

Brown, L. B., "Race as a Factor in Establishing a Casework Relationship." *Social Casework*, Vol. 31, 1950, pp. 91–97.

Broyard, A., "Portrait of the Inauthentic Negro: How Prejudice Distorts the Victim's Personality." *Commentary*, Vol. 10, 1950, pp. 56–64.

Buchheimer, A., and Balogh, S. C., *The Counseling Relationship*. Chicago: Science Research Associates, 1961.

Clark, K. B., "The Negro Is Tired of Waiting." *U.S. News and World Report*, June 10, 1963, pp. 38–40.

Clark, K. B., and Plotkin, L., *The Negro Student at Integrated Colleges*. New York: National Scholarship and Service Fund for Negro Students, 1963.

Cohen, Marcel, *Pour une Sociologie du Langage*. Paris: Editions Albins Michel, 1956.

Cothran, T. C., "Negro Conceptions of White People." *American Journal of Sociology*, Vol. 56, 1951, pp. 458–467.

Crites, J. O., *Vocational Psychology*. New York: McGraw-Hill, 1969.

Cronbach, L. J., *Essentials of Psychological Testing*, 2nd ed. New York: Harper and Brothers, 1960.

Dai, B., "Some Problems of Personality Development among Negro Children." In C. Kluckhohn and H. A. Murray (Eds.), *Personality in Nature, Society, and Culture*, 2nd ed. New York: Alfred A. Knopf, 1953.

Devine, D., "Coeducation: A Contributing Factor in Miseducation of the Disadvantaged." *Phi Delta Kappan*, Vol. 46, 1964, pp. 126–128.

Fanon, F., *Black Skin, White Masks*. New York: Grove Press, 1967.

Fibush, E., "The White Worker and the Negro Client." *Social Casework*, Vol. 46, 1965, pp. 271–277.

Frazier, E. F., *The Negro in the United States*, rev. ed. New York: Macmillan, 1960.

Goff, R. M., "Problems and Emotional Difficulties of Negro Children Due to Race." *Journal of Negro Education*, Vol. 19, 1950, pp. 152–158.

Greenson, R. R., *The Technique and Practice of Psychoanalysis*, Vol. I, 2nd ed. New York: International Universities Press, 1967.

Grier, W. H., and Cobbs, P. M., *Black Rage*. New York: Basic Books, 1968.

Hare, N., *The Black Anglo-Saxons*. New York: Marzani and Munsell, 1965.

Harrington, M., "The Economics of Protest." In A. M. Rose and H. Hill (Eds.), *Employment, Race, and Poverty*. New York: Harcourt, Brace and World, 1967.

Harrison, S. I., and Carek, D. J., *A Guide to Psychotherapy*. Boston: Little, Brown and Co., 1966.

Havighurst, R. J., *Human Development in Education*. New York: David McKay, 1953.

Heine, R. W., "Negro Patient in Psychotherapy." *Journal of Clinical Psychology*, Vol. 6, 1950, pp. 373–376.

Himes, J. S., "The Negro Teen-age Culture." *Annals of the American Academy of Political and Social Sciences*, Vol. 338, 1961, pp. 91–101.

Hinsie, L. E., and Campbell, R. J., *Psychiatric Dictionary*, 3rd ed. New York: Oxford University Press, 1960.

Holland, J. H., "Educational Implications behind the Racial Wall." *Journal of the Association of College Admissions Counselors*, Vol. 10, 1964, pp. 13–17.

———, "Negro and Higher Education." *NEA Journal*, Vol. 54, 1965, pp. 22–24.

Jourard, S. M., "Healthy Personality and Self-disclosure." *Mental Hygiene*, Vol. 43, 1959, pp. 499–509.

———, "Age Trends in Self-disclosure." *Merrill-Palmer Quarterly*, Vol. 7, 1961, pp. 191–197.

———, *The Transparent Self*. Princeton, N.J.: D. Van Nostrand, 1964.

———, and Lasakow, P., "Some Factors in Self-disclosure." *Journal of Abnormal and Social Psychology*, Vol. 56, 1958, pp. 91–98.

Kalish, C. B., "A Portrait of the Unemployed." *Monthly Labor Review*, Vol. 89, 1966, pp. 7–14.

Karon, B. P., *The Negro Personality*. New York: Springer, 1958.

Keller, S., "The Social World of the Urban Slum Child: Some Early Findings." *American Journal of Orthopsychiatry*, Vol. 33, 1963, pp. 823–831.

Killian, L., and Grigg, C., *Racial Crisis in America*. Englewood Cliffs, N.J.: Prentice-Hall, 1964.

Kohn, M. L., "Social Class and Parent-Child Relationships: An Interpretation." *American Journal of Sociology*, Vol. 68, 1963, pp. 471–480.

Landsman, T., "Role of Self-concept in Learning Situations." *High School Journal*, Vol. 45, 1962, pp. 289–295.

Lazarus, R. S., *Personality and Adjustment*. Englewood Cliffs, N.J.: Prentice-Hall, 1963.

Lee, A. M., *Multivalent Man*. New York: George Braziller, 1966.

Lefcourt, H. M., "Some Empirical Correlates of Negro Identity." Unpublished doctoral dissertation, Ohio State University, 1963.

MacIver, R. M., and Page, C. H., *Society*. New York: Rinehart, 1949.

Mehrens, W. A., and Lehmann, I. J, *Standardized Tests in Education*. New York: Rinehart and Winston, 1969.

Middleton, R., "Alienation, Race, and Education." *American Sociological Review*, Vol. 28, 1963, pp. 973–977.

Milner, E., "Some Hypotheses Concerning the Influence of Segregation on Negro Personality Development." *Psychiatry*, Vol. 16, 1953, pp. 291–297.

Patterson, C. H., "Client Expectations and Social Conditioning." *Personnel and Guidance Journal*, Vol. 37, 1958, pp. 136–138.

————, *Theories of Counseling and Psychotherapy*. New York: Harper and Row, 1966.

Phillips, R. E., "Firstborn in the North." *Educational Leadership*, Vol. 26, 1968, pp. 21–23.

Record, W., "Counseling and Communication." *Journal of Negro Education*, Vol. 30, 1961, pp. 450–454.

Riessman, F., "The Overlooked Positives of Disadvantaged Groups." *Journal of Negro Education*, Vol. 34, 1965, pp. 160–166.

Rogers, C. R., "The Characteristics of a Helping Relationship." *Personnel and Guidance Journal*, Vol. 37, 1958, pp. 6–16.

————, "The Interpersonal Relationship: The Core of Guidance." *Harvard Educational Review*, Vol. 32, 1962, pp. 416–429.

Rose, A. M., *The Negro's Morale*. Minneapolis: University of Minnesota Press, 1949.

Sarvis, M. A., "Evil Self-image: A Common Denominator in Learning Problems." *Mental Hygiene*, Vol. 49, 1965, pp. 308–310.

Shertzer, B., and Peters, H. J., *Guidance: Techniques for Industrial Appraisal and Development*. New York: Macmillan, 1965.

———, and Stone, S. C., "School Counselor and his Publics: A Problem in Role Definition." *Personnel and Guidance Journal*, Vol. 41, 1963, pp. 687–693.

———, and Stone, S. C., *Fundamentals of Counseling*. Boston: Houghton Mifflin, 1968.

Society for the Psychological Study of Social Issues, "Guidelines for Testing Minority Group Children." *Journal of Social Issues*, Vol. 20, 1964, (Supplement), pp. 127–145.

Sprey, J., "Sex Differences in Occupational Choice Patterns among Negro Adolescents." *Social Problems*, Vol. 10, 1962, pp. 11–23.

Super, D. E., and Crites, J. O., *Appraising Vocational Fitness*, rev. ed. New York: Harper and Row, 1962.

Swinehart, J. W., "Socio-economic Level, Status Aspirations, and Maternal Role." *American Sociological Review*, Vol. 28, 1963, pp. 391–399.

Thompson, D. C., "Development of Attitudes in Respect to Discrimination." *American Journal of Orthopsychiatry*, Vol. 32, 1962, pp. 74–85.

Trent, R. D., "The Color of the Investigator as a Variable in Experimental Research with Negro Subjects." *Journal of Social Psychology*, Vol. 40, 1954, pp. 281–287.

———, "Relation between Expressed Self-acceptance and Expressed Attitudes toward Negroes and Whites among Negro Children." *Journal of Genetic Psychology*, Vol. 91, 1957, pp. 25–31.

Trueblood, D. L., "Role of the Counselor in the Guidance of Negro Students." *Harvard Educational Review*, Vol. 30, 1960, pp. 252–269.

Tuma, A. H., and Gustad, J. W., "The Effects of Client and Counselor Personality Characteristics on Client Learning in Counseling." *Journal of Counseling Psychology*, Vol. 4, 1957, pp. 136–141.

Vontress, C. E., "The Negro Personality Reconsidered." *Journal of Negro Education*, Vol. 35, 1966, pp. 210–217.

———, "Counseling the Culturally Different in our Society." *Journal of Employment Counseling*, Vol. 6, 1969, pp. 9–16. (a)

———, "Cultural Barriers in the Counseling Relationship." *Personnel and Guidance Journal*, Vol. 48, 1969, pp. 11–17. (b)

———, "Counseling Blacks." *Personnel and Guidance Journal*, Vol. 48, 1970, pp. 713–719.

White, R. W., *The Abnormal Personality*, 2nd ed. New York: Ronald Press, 1948.

Woods, F. J., "Cultural Conditioning and Mental Health." *Social Casework*, Vol. 39, 1958, pp. 327–333.

Wright, S. J., "The Negro College in America." *Harvard Educational Review*, Vol. 30, 1960, pp. 280–297.

INDEX

Achievement, need for, 21
Aggressive counseling, 22–23
Ambivalence of blacks toward whites, 35
Black, defined, 1–2
Black adolescents, 10
Black bourgeois parents, 30–31
Black college administrators, 38
Black college students, 29–35
Black counselors, 41
Black culture, 53–54
Black male, 49–50
Black matriarchy, 10
Black middle-class family, 11–12
Black studies, 36–37
College admissions, 23
College admissions representatives, 23–24
College counseling, 17–25
College counselor, role of, 36, 38
Colored, defined, 2
Congruence, 43
Constructs, diagnostic, 2
Counseling, defined, 1, 60
Counseling interview, 46
Counselor as consultant, 38
Counselor attitudes, 42
Counselor training, 61–63
Countertransference, 51–52
Cultural differences, 53
Discrimination, 16
Drug use among black college students, 31–32
Empathy, 43
Financial assistance for college, 26
"Great white father syndrome," 52
Guidance, defined, 62
Hostility of blacks toward whites, 48–49
Identity crisis among black college students, 33
Intelligence tests, 55–56
Interest, defined, 57
Interest inventories, 57–58
Interracial colleges, 26

Lower-class black parents, 31
Masculine protest in black males, 32
Matriarchy, the black, 34
Middle-class black parents, 30–31
Middle-class students, 21
National Achievement Scholarship Program for Negro Students, 26
National Scholarship Service and Fund for Negro Students, 26
Negro adults, 39
Negro college students, 25
Negro colleges, 24–25, 37
Negro counselors, 44
Negro girls, 11
Negro mothers, 9
Negro personality, 57
Negro students, 15
Negro teachers, 12, 25
Negro teenage culture, 9
Negro youth, characteristics of, 9
  attitudes toward white teachers, 10
Pay-as-you-go college plans, 18
Personality tests, 56–57
Positive regard, 44
Proficiency tests, 55
Racial secrets, 7–8
Racial separatism, 54
Rapport, 39–40, 60–61
  and age of counselor, 42
  and self-disclosure, 42
  and sex of the counselor, 40–41
  defined, 4, 39
  establishing of, 46
  with adults, 39
Reaction formation, 30, 34
Reflection, 50–51
Resistance, 49–50
School principal, 13
Self-concept, 10, 29
Self-disclosure, 7
Sensitivity training, 62
"Soul," defined, 3
Structuring the counseling relationship, 47

7587 5 am ¥